FREE
HAND-
NEW
TYPO-
GRAPHY
SKETCH-
BOOKS

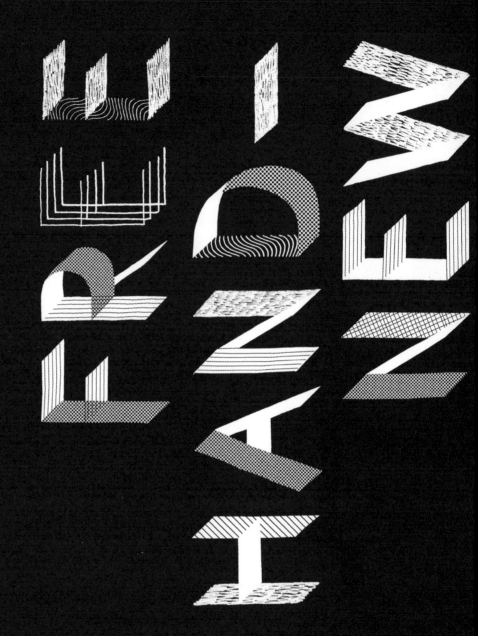

Abrams, New York

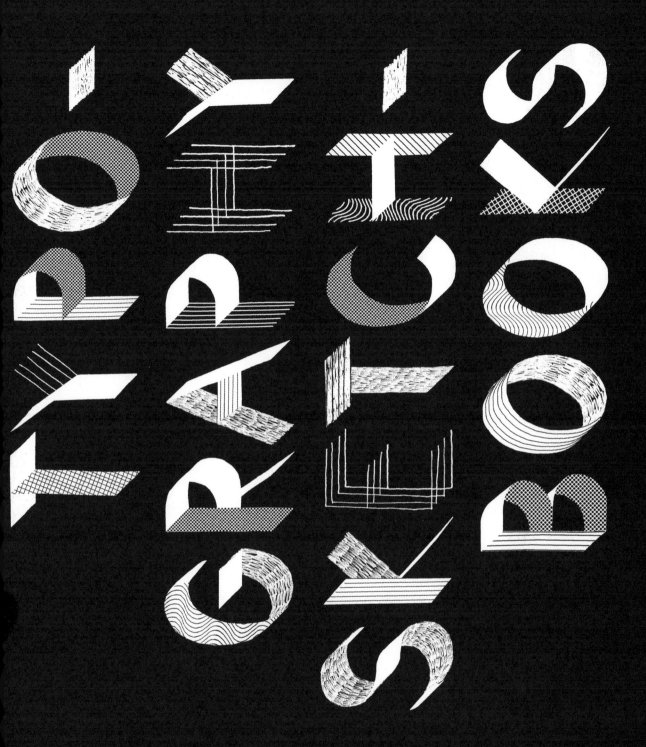

TYPOGRAPHY SKETCHBOOKS

Steven Heller & Lita Talarico

with over 800 illustrations

Contents

LETTER-ING IN THE RAW

DIREC-TORY

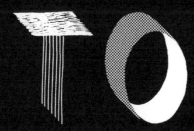

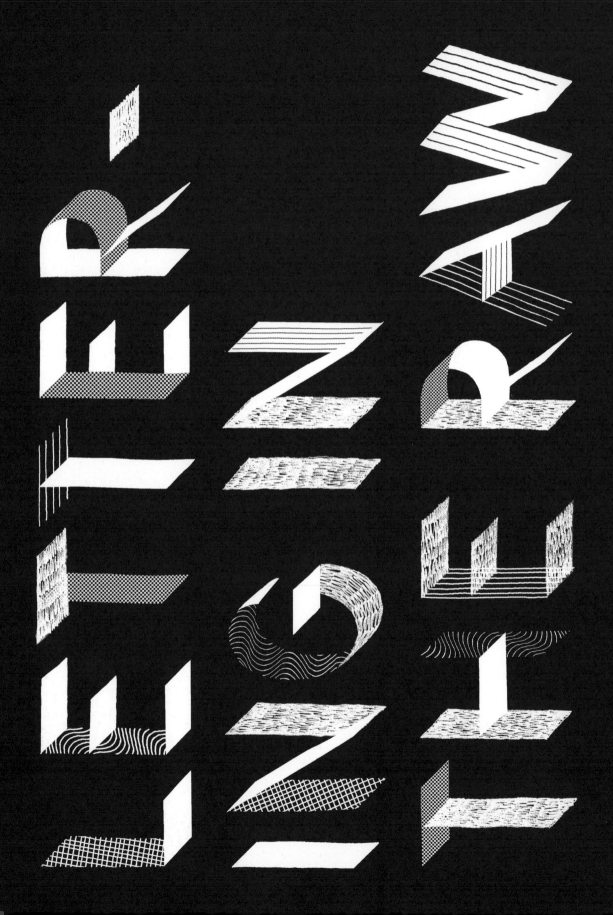

rawing letters is quite possibly one of life's most joyful pleasures – for a designer, at least, it had better be. Even for a non-designer, letters have allure. Letterforms are both abstract and representational, sculptural and painterly. There are infinite ways to draw Latin, Blackletter, Arabic, Hebrew and Cyrillic characters, not to mention the Chinese, Japanese and Korean symbols among the huge number of pictographic forms. Sketching literal forms in unconventional ways challenges the common standards of universal comprehension. Toying with legibility pushes the boundaries of readability. Lettering in the raw is not just instructive, it's fun.

Of course, type is meant to be read – or deciphered – not just looked at and admired. But reading can be a visceral, as well as an intellectual experience. Often interpreting the letters is as emotional a process as it is cognitive. Naturally, experimental lettering can be distracting if it is employed on a legal document or an instructional guide. Don't try it with a tax form or voting ballot. Yet lettering for so many things, from advertisements and signs to book and magazine texts, might benefit from distinctive, even puzzling, typography.

This is why maintaining sketchbooks – or, indeed, randomly scrawling on any blank surface – is not just liberating, it is also useful. Finding new ways to communicate ideas by experimenting with different means of representing letters increases a designer's opportunities for expression. It is clear from the sketches in this book that approaches to playing with type and letters appear to be infinite. From the restrained to the incredible, type designers value the opportunity to toy with the written word.

One reason for this is the welcome inclusion of more non-Latin designs. Over the past two decades the commercial demand for Arabic type and typography has exponentially increased as Middle Eastern countries have played larger roles on the world stage. Indeed, an increasing amount of Western design schools have opened campuses in these countries, which has led to greater interest in how Latin lettering traditions have affected Arabic approaches. The growing influence of Arabic type is not limited to the Middle East or even to Middle Eastern designers; an exciting typographic internationalism has arisen in font foundries and design studios around the world.

A generous helping of non-Latin sketching contributes to the otherworldly quality of this book. Books and exhibits emerging from Western countries have long ignored or marginalized those that appear not to have typographic relevance. But as design becomes a more globalized discipline, and non-Latin writers take their rightful place on the world stage, linguistic diversity is growing.

Beyond the practical need for new type and typographies, there is a pleasure in experimenting with new and exotic letters in typography, which are a joy for the eye. Most Western designers will never actually understand Arabic or Farsi, but the aesthetic wonderment that we derive from transforming these characters into typographic pictures brings us closer to these languages.

As more and more designers become engaged with type design, the goal of this book is to expose new faces (human, that is) to its joys. It is never dull to see what designers and illustrators get up to – on sketch paper – when nobody is looking. Although some prefer not to show this raw, informal and free output, plenty more have opened their files, closets and bookshelves to our persistent requests. To all of them, thank you.

Steven Heller & Lita Talarico

Majid Abbasi
Toronto • Ontario • Canada

'Sketches are the basis of my design,' says art director and senior design consultant Majid Abbasi, co-editor of the Iranian design magazine *Neshan* and founder of Studio Abbasi, with offices in Tehran and Toronto. 'Sometimes the form will change a little during the process, but not in terms of content. Seeing what happens during the sketch amazes me.'

Majid is always discovering new forms, and draws using pen and paper, the Figure app on his iPad, or a mouse and a computer. He does almost all of his sketching on pieces of paper, sometimes on bits of tissue, and sometimes in his diary. In other words, he says, 'I do not have organized sketchbooks.'

In 2013 Majid designed a new cover for Heinrich Boll's novel *The Bread of Those Early Years* (1955), a love story set during the Second World War. 'The first idea for the cover was a loaf of bread, which is transformed into the shape of a heart – the universal symbol of love,' he explains. 'I went to the bakery and bought a loaf of bread, and then came back to the studio and played around with the slices. I discovered that I could place two of them in opposite directions to each other, and there was no need to photomontage the result. For me, the result was more impressive and amazing than anything Photoshop could produce.'

Coca Albers
New York • New York • USA

Brazilian-born graphic designer and illustrator Coca Albers claims that she cannot start a project without sketching or drawing her ideas. The process of doing so, she says, is essential to the finished work. 'Sketching has a very strong impact on my work, because I have more control over the idea when I'm drawing,' she explains. 'What I like most about it is the freedom.'

Coca's habit is to keep everything in her sketchbook, but, she admits, 'I also end up using a lot of clean surfaces that I find along the way.' Among her favourite materials are – what else? – 'sharpened pencils and Muji pens'.

Having designed branding and exhibitions for museums (the Museum of Tomorrow in Rio de Janeiro and the Museum of Portuguese Language in São Paulo among them) and worked in product development for fashion labels (including C&A and Cavalera), Coca is currently based in New York, studying typography design at the Cooper Union.

+ CONDENSED

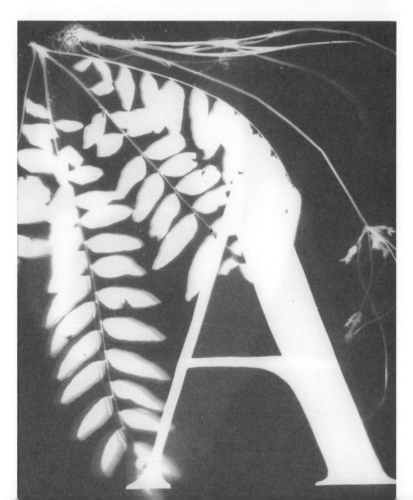

Kelli Anderson

Brooklyn • New York • USA

'I like to sketch to gain certainty about a hunch,' says artist, designer and self-confessed 'tinkerer' Kelli Anderson. 'I often cut out and arrange paper, rather than drawing directly onto it. Working in this way helps give a feeling of mystery and possibility to the process, because I can never fully visualize the subtle complexity that light and shadow brings. This makes it more fun and exciting.'

Occasionally the experiment can be controlled, and turns out more or less as expected. 'Sometimes it takes a turn, which is definitely annoying for the task at hand,' she adds, 'but it can usually be recycled for another project later.'

For the paper-lettering project *Carl Sagan* (p. 20), Kelli employed a technique that failed to yield an appropriate logo design, but worked great as an animated title card for a trippy quote from the late astronomer. 'Letting in a little daylight is very helpful,' Kelli notes. 'I find more possibilities outside of my mind than in it.'

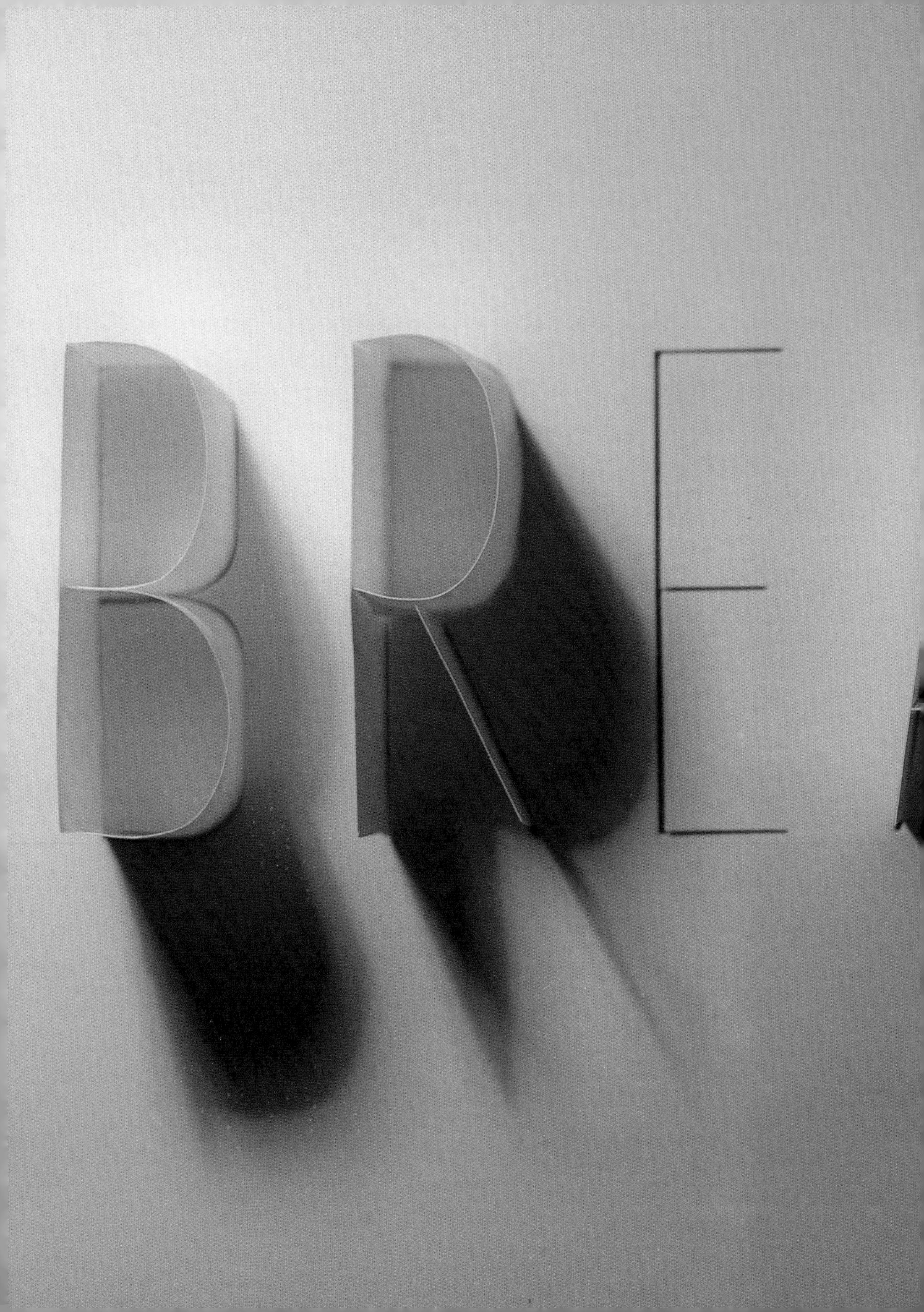
BRE

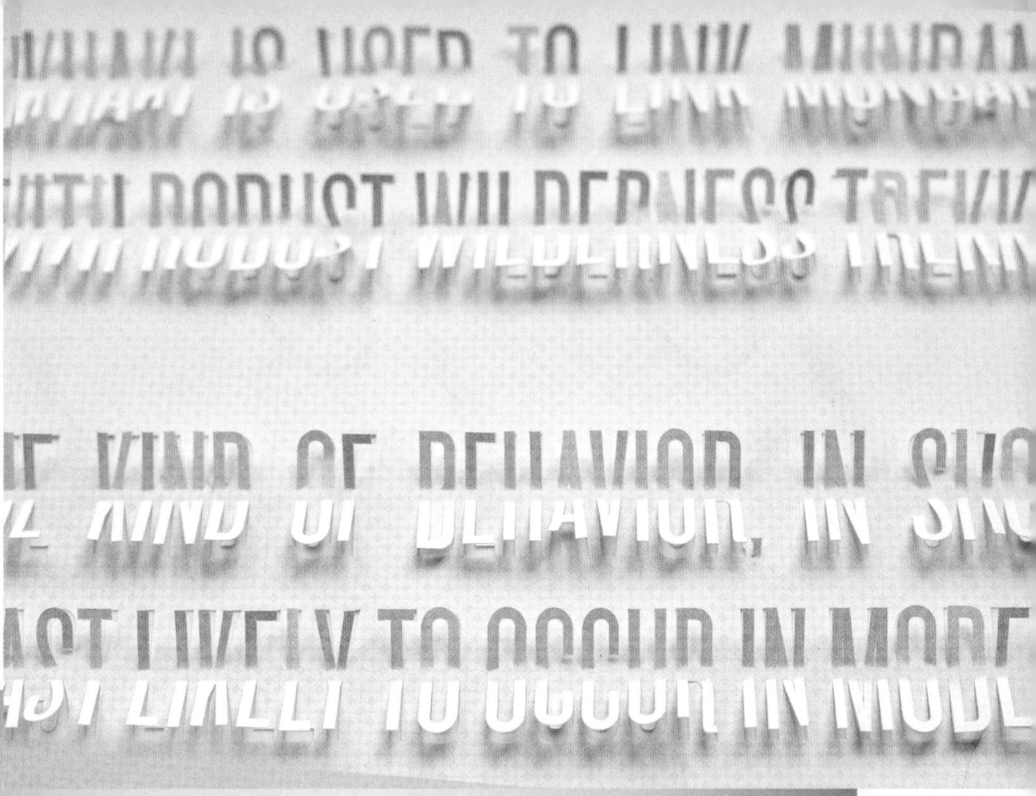

WHICH IS USED TO LINK MUNDAN

WITH ROBUST WILDERNESS TREKKI

E KIND OF BEHAVIOR, IN SHO

AST LIKELY TO OCCUR IN MODE

WHAT ELSE CAN WE DO WITH

WHAT ELSE CAN WE DO WITH

THESE EXPECTATIONS?

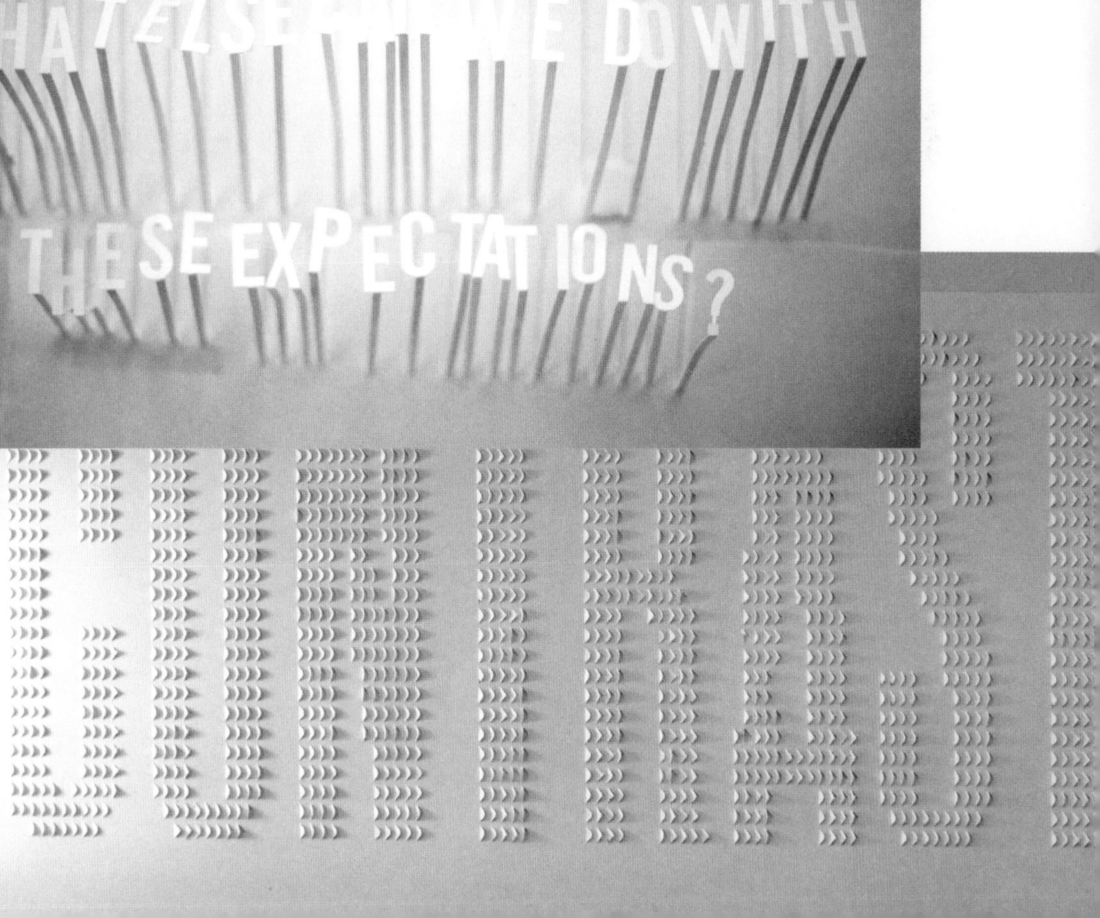

Philippe Apeloig

Paris • France

Graphic designer and typographer Philippe Apeloig has had a distinguished career: he has collaborated with the likes of Jean Nouvel, two recent exhibitions (at the Musée des Arts Décoratifs in Paris and the Stedelijk Museum in Amsterdam) have been devoted to his work, and his designs are in the permanent collection of the Museum of Modern Art in New York.

Sketching, Philippe says, is a 'doorway through which I can develop and unfold an idea, put it into form and visually challenge it. When I take on a job, I focus my thoughts, but words, images, text, music, all kinds of things float by me. I never have preconceived ideas, as that would mean inventing a visual to translate them. Sketches of letters and shapes begin to pile up. I change elements, and everything moves.

I have to work with constraints – the number of letters in a word or title, for example.'

About the sketching process, he says, 'I have used computers since the earliest years of digital media, but I have kept up the practice of drawing on paper. This allows me to jump from one tool to the other easily, and thanks to the printer I can scribble over a sketch done on the computer.'

Curiously, Philippe likens sketching to gambling: 'I work with the luck of the drawing. The letter arrangements that I try out, the ones that impose themselves, end up taking the right form – the correct form, in my eyes. That's when the searching stops, at the pivotal point, supported by what becomes a mass of preparatory sketches. That's when I can go and show it to the client, justifying it if necessary.'

Philippe enjoys the hesitations, the research, the experimentation, the unknown and the back and forth between pencil, screen and paper. It's all about 'the speed of sketching, the freedom given by a pencil over a blank sheet of paper,' he concludes. 'Drawing is also thinking, evolving one's reflection.'

D&A

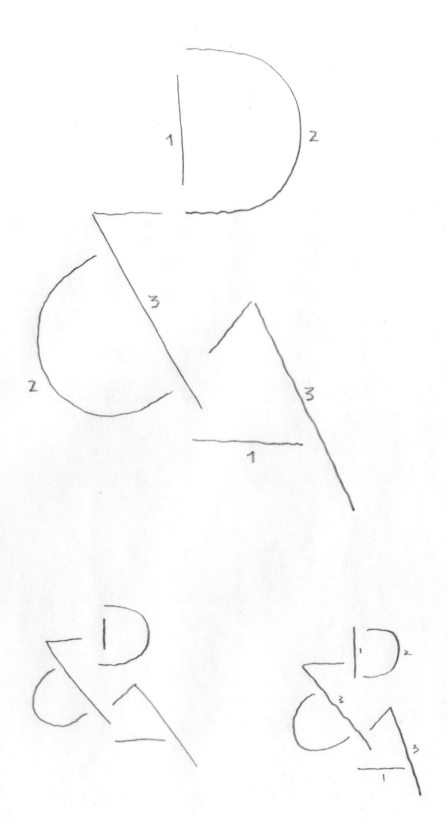

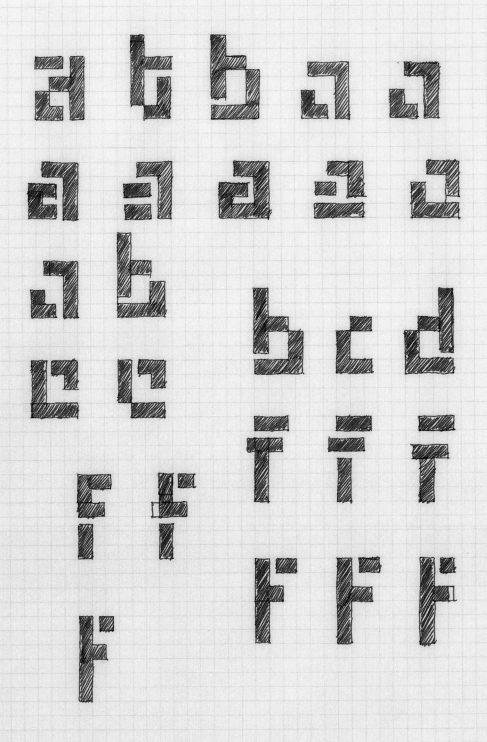

Andrea Arcangeli

Rome • Italy

Sketching is integral to every type-based project that freelance calligrapher Andrea Arcangeli takes on. 'I usually begin by sketching ideas with a pencil, before moving to pen on paper, and finally to the computer for refinements,' he says. 'It is the most important part of a design, and requires a lot of concentration.'

Sketching is also a difficult and important part of the calligraphy process. 'I usually decide the spacings and begin sketching the forms as precisely as I can,' Andrea explains, 'using plenty of geometry and grids to make the pen and ink part as easy as possible.'

With his graphic-designer hat on, Andrea sketches more loosely. There is no need for meticulous work, as the computer programs he uses will allow small modifications to the finished article.

Andrea has had a computer at home since the age of 13, and as a child acquired a 'passion for hand-drawn graphics that later developed into a passion for letters'. At university, while the other students were working entirely at the computer, Andrea would develop projects by sketching, and then refining his drawings on the computer. Since then, he says, 'I have learned to use the computer only when necessary.'

For the wedding invitations of two marines in the Italian armed forces, Andrea was asked by the couple for a monogram design that would suggest both the sea and the idea of the infinite, with their initials inside.

'I used a fine-pointed nib for the letters, so they could be modified to be perfectly symmetrical,' Andrea explains. 'I added a swash to form a sailor knot, a symbol of union and, more graphically, of infinity. Then I cleaned up the form to make it become, on the computer, an ambigram. The couple were thrilled with the final design – love at first sight!'

The Darkne[ss]
characters o[f]
the whitene[ss]
P

s of the

erpowers

s of the

Tarek Atrissi

Barcelona • Spain

'There is no way of creating a solid design without going through a certain amount of experimentation,' says type designer Tarek Atrissi. 'On the one hand, sketching can help to conceptualize a project, and on the other, a concept can never be refined without sketching to help validate and finalize it.'

Tarek, an early advocate of new Arabic type, notes that sketches help when trying to convince clients. 'Walking the clients through the sketching process shows them how the design was created, and how much trial and error goes on behind the scenes,' he says. 'That's why I always integrate a number of sketches into any presentation.'

Tarek and his team were tasked by the city of Abu Dhabi with designing an Arabic digital typeface that would recreate the handwriting of Sheikh Zayed bin Khalifa Al Nahyan (1840–1909), the founder and first president of the United Arab Emirates.

'We were given letters written by Zayed over a hundred years ago,' Tarek explains. 'We mixed old and new for the final result, in which the historic "sketchbooks" were the basis for further development and new sketching to revive the spirit of the lettering style.'

Some Arabic typefaces designed by Tarek were created entirely by sketching the letterforms. Others were designed on the computer, including the initial conceptualizing phase, but sketching – in whatever form – is always at the essence of the design process.

'It reminds me of my years studying at various design schools,' Tarek says. 'Sketching is an experimental process that will always bring unexpected results.'

Peter Bankov

Moscow · Russia

'The thing I like most about drawing is the freedom,' says graphic designer Peter Bankov. 'I like working with ink and using the methods of Constructivism and Russian calligraphy of the pre-Peter the Great (1672–1725) era.'

Peter started out as a sculptor, before becoming a book illustrator and designer, and finds inspiration in the work of the Futurists and Dadaists. Of his working practice, he says, 'I make small sketches, and then draw fonts and pictures in large format, before taking photos and producing the final image on the computer.'

He also, rather enterprisingly, makes his own brushes from newspapers and paper. 'I make a roll, cut down one side and a primitive brush appears,' he says. 'I also use wooden sticks, flattening one end with a hammer, toothbrushes and cotton buds.'

When Peter took on some students from South Korea for calligraphy lessons in his studio, they were horrified. 'In their opinion,' he explains, 'a true calligrapher must meditate, and only then begin creating. Seeing me, they thought that my calligraphy must be both awful and wonderful, and against the laws of great art.'

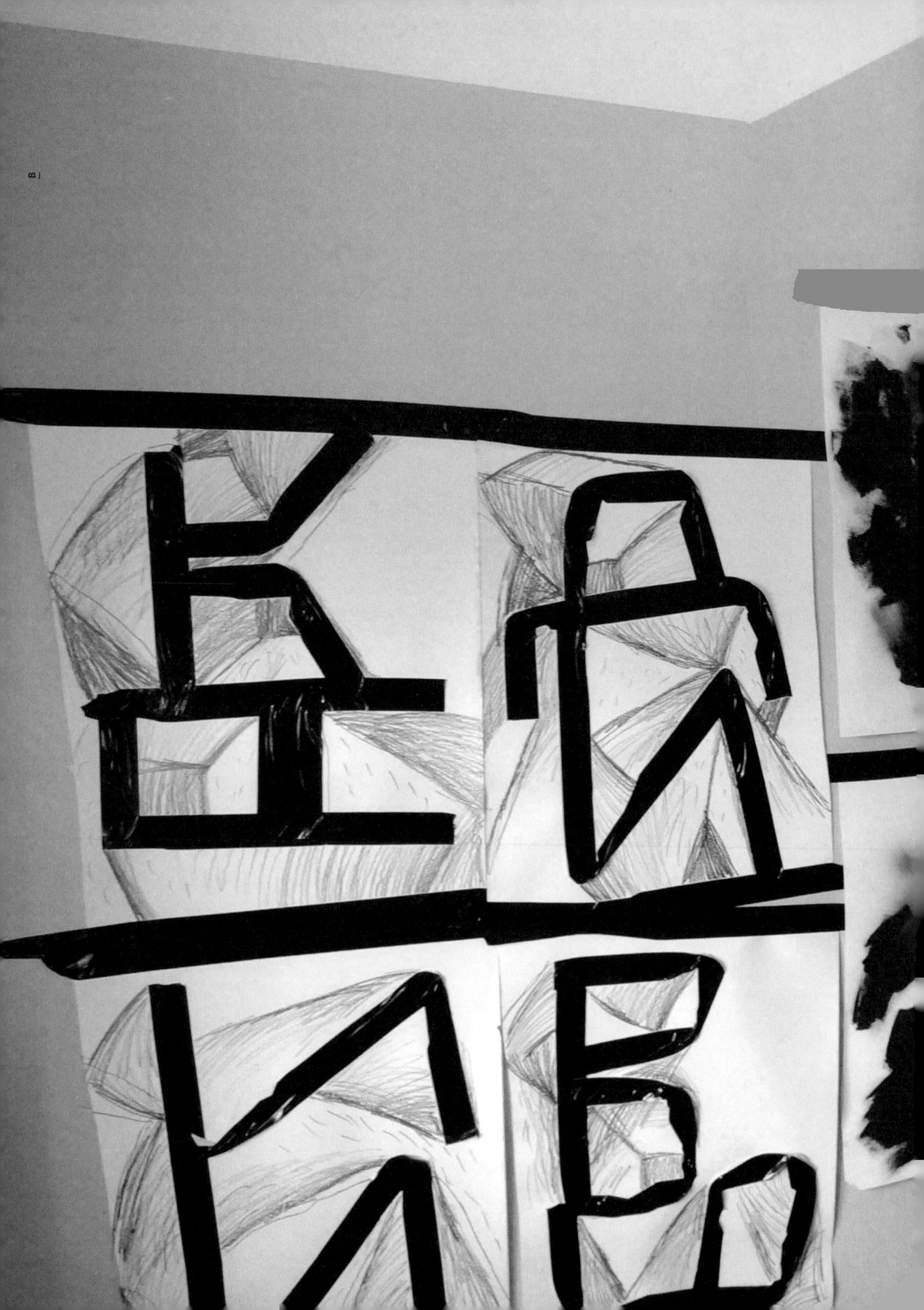

8

Gabriel Benderski

Montevideo · Uruguay

'Going around with my pad and pen is second nature,' says graphic designer Gabriel Benderski. 'Having a notebook with me allows me to open my mind, feel creative and distil an idea into a visual solution in any place, at any time. When I buy a pair of trousers, I even check to see if it will fit in the pocket.'

Sketching also allows Gabriel to dig deeper and eliminate the obvious. 'You never know what will inspire you,' he says. 'You jump from one idea to the next, one of which could spark the very concept you were looking for. You also need to be mentally prepared to face a blank page. Shall I disturb its whiteness with a stroke of my pen? Will it ruin the purity or will it help the page to have more personality?'

Gabriel does not have a preferred tool. 'When I sketch,' he says, 'I like to try and change the instrument I am using. Different pens produce different strokes or writing speeds, for example. This game of playing with pens has significant consequences: I see it as an advantage that helps me produce richer, more versatile ideas when I am looking for a concept. The main reason why I go out and buy a notebook is because it assures me that all of my messy drawings will be in one place, and that they will be together forever.'

GRIS
MARRON
luciernaga
HAA
aguerrebere
AGUER
AGUERR
Aguerrebere

212-175-55
montevideo
URUGUAY
TAGA TREND AND SAY IT WISH STYLE
MOTHERFUCKER
BITCH
MANHATTAN
BASTARD
NOT INSPIRATION
AMSTERDAM BERLIN URUGUAY
PORNOGRAPHY
MARIJUANA
NEWYORK

Ed Benguiat

New York • New York • USA

Ed Benguiat, the legendary typographer and lettering artist, is known for many things, from his over 600 generation-defining typefaces (of which ITC Benguiat, Tiffany and Souvenir are just three) to removing the full stop from the *New York Times* masthead. Many of his typefaces were originally created for Photo Lettering, the company founded in 1936

by Edward Rondthaler, who would later go on to set up the International Type Company with the equally legendary graphic designer Herb Lubalin.

Ed designed and redesigned the logotypes for *Esquire, McCall's, Reader's Digest, Photography, Look, Sports Illustrated, The Star Ledger, The San Diego Tribune*, AT&T, Estée Lauder, and many more. Together with Lubalin, he contributed to the development of the influential typographic journal *U&lc*.

'Too many people think that if they have a computer, they can draw a logo or a typeface,' Ed noted in 2000,

on the occasion of his induction into the Art Directors Club Hall of Fame. 'You have to learn to draw first. The computer won't do it for you.' As the technology improved, however, Ed became more optimistic about computer-assisted type design.

The sketches shown here are from the School of Visual Arts Milton Glaser Archive, and show the precision that imbues everything Ed touches – as well as the incomparable skill he has with a white-out brush.

5 59%

774

TP. 50% E.B

OT

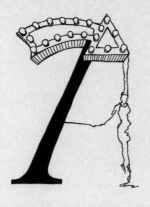

ARROWS AND ARTISTS

BROOKLYN BRIDGE

CENTRAL PARK

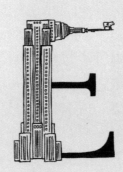

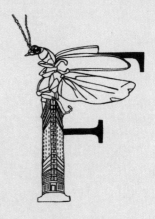

DINER AND DONUT

EMPIRE STATE

FIREFLY AND FLATIRON

ICECREAM

JAZZ AND JEWS

KITE AND KETCHUP

ZOO

Julie Bjørnskov

Copenhagen · Denmark

'I love to illustrate life's little moments, and give them a twist of magic and abstraction,' says Julie Bjørnskov, describing the process of drawing in general and lettering specifically.

Julie, a graphic designer and illustrator who works in Copenhagen as an interactive designer, tries to show in her work the beauty of everyday life by 'combining typography and illustration, and giving every letter its own story and mood'. The alphabet illustrated here was inspired by a summer spent in New York while attending the Type As Language residency programme at the School of Visual Arts.

'I drew these sketches when I returned to Copenhagen,' she says, 'inspired by the amazing experience of the programme and the city.'

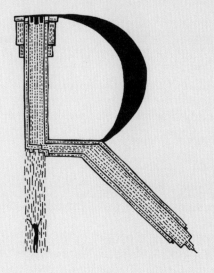

ROCKEFELLER RAIN

STATUE OF LIBERTY

TIMES SQUARE

UMBRELLA AND UNIFORM

VINTAGE VILLAGE VANGUARD

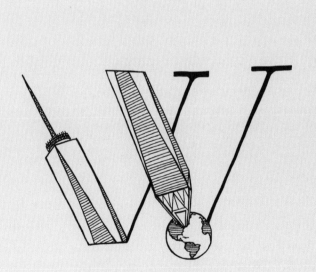

WORLD TRADE CENTER

XOBMOOB // BOOMBOX

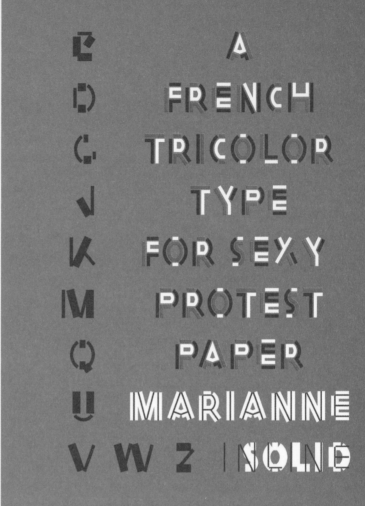

Benoît Bodhuin

Nantes · France

Designer and typographer Benoît Bodhuin, the founder of typeface company BB Bureau, always has a sheet of paper beside him for jotting down ideas and sketches on the go. 'These drawings are very far from the finished result, however,' he explains. 'They sit somewhere between aide-mémoire and formal research.'

The ways in which these loose arrangements of letters assist Benoît in deciding on a final typeface vary from project to project. 'Sometimes the requirements imposed on the design dictate the outcome,' he says. 'At other times I just play on a single criterion, such as pitch or darkness of the letter. There are occasions when you have to modify the design of the letter, and that's when I scribble on my sheet.'

Benoît goes back and forth between working sketches out on draft paper and creating approximate vector drawings. For his 'Pipo' typeface, sketching allowed him to develop more glyphs and greater difference between weights and other nuanced changes.

MARIANE

(CAPS) MADE UP OF TAPE MODULES.

LINE TYPEFACE EXISTING IN 3 STYLES — INLINE, SOLID ET OUTLINE.
...ANNE IS DESIGNED BY BENOÎT BODHUIN
...YLES

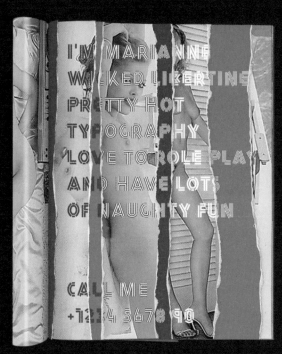

I'M MARIANNE
WICKED LIBERTINE
PRETTY HOT
TYPOGRAPHY
LOVE TO ROLE PLAY
AND HAVE LOTS
OF NAUGHTY FUN

CALL ME
+1234 5678 90

ladies and gentlemen, on behalf of the crew, we wish

to welcome on board this Aircaster Flight. We will be

attending to your safety and comfort during this Flight

All mobile phones should be in airplane mode. Please

fasten your seat belt securely. Emergency exits

on either side of the cabin are clearly marked by EXIT

sign. Floor lighting will guide you to these exits

In case of an emergency you will have to leave your

luggage in the plane. If there is a drop in cabin

pressure your oxygen mask will automatically drop down

in front of you. Pull the mask to release the oxygen

Benoît Bodhuin - impression Lézard Graphique - typographie Side A - n° 7

Place the mask over your nose and mouth and breath

normally. Sun will find these safety precautions in

seat pocket in front of you. Please read it carefully

Bestandteile der großen Baukunst.

seiner Hand erblühen, die Grundlage des Werkmäßigen aber ist unerläßlich
zeichner und Kunstgewerbler muß endlich wieder eine bauende
...en Sie
Wenn der
erst
verspürt,
Bres A
zu erle
untere
errei
hr zu un
Masse
Zukun
ir bleibt
esamt
ermag.
begrei
k zurück
Werk
esensun

C'est nous, artistes, qui
servirons d'avant-garde:
puissance des arts est e
la plus immédiate et
rapide. Nous avons
toute espèce: quand
voulons répandre des
neuves parmi les ho
les inscrivons sur l
sur la toile... Quelle
des
d'ex
puis
sac
ava
inte
plus

Claude Henri de Rouvroy

Depuis 1913, nous ressentions tous un besoin d'abstraction et de simplification. Le caractère mathématiq... toute évidence face à l'impressionnisme, que nous rejetions: tout ce qui n'allait pas au bout de nos princ... qualifié de "baroque". Nous étions tous d'accord sur un point: nous déclarions la guerre au style baroque... Formes les plus diverses. Theo van Doesburg

L'architect
doit créer
des formes
qui support
la répétiti
Marcel Bre

Une grande époque vient de commencer. Il existe un esprit nouveau. Il existe une foule d'œuvres d'esprit nouveau: elles se rencontrent surtout dans la production industrielle. L'architecture étouffe dans les usages. Les styles sont un mensonge. Le style, c'est une unité de principe qui anime toutes les œuvres d'une époque et qui résulte d'un esprit caractérisé. Notre époque fixe chaque jour son style. Nos yeux, malheureusement, ne savent pas le discerner enco... Le Corbusier

Le Style, a
Racine, c'es
pensée exp
avec le min
de mots. L
Style en ar
tecture, c'
pensée exp
suivant les
naturelles
l'économie
noblesse de
structure.

Auguste Perret

ard Fritz Aingaster-Fuchs

Sophie Elinor Brown

Newcastle • New South Wales Australia

The repetitive nature of sketching 'makes me creatively fit', says graphic designer, radio producer and self-titled 'type dork' Sophie Elinor Brown. 'In a pragmatic sense, it helps me to progress ideas forward. But more romantically, sketching archives slices of time. Perhaps I'm just more of an analogue, tactile kind of person, but I never leaf through old digital files in the same way I do finished sketchbooks.'

If she hadn't spent years scribbling away with brushes and pens, Sophie says,

she would be 'absolutely clueless' about letterforms. 'The piles of old sketchbooks on my shelves are the classrooms in which I learned the fundamentals of form, balance, curves and rhythm,' she explains. 'The process of drawing over and over lends a level of authenticity to all of my digital and illustrative work.'

Lately she has tried pushing her lettering in a more pictorial direction: 'I'm a bit of a sucker for punishment, so the more intricate a design is, the more I enjoy it. A wedding invitation I designed involved days of precisely tessellating stippled drawings of animals, so that the negative space around them spelled out the couple's names. It seems like a logistical nightmare, but I found the process quite therapeutic.'

it's not
~ROCKET~
surgery

IT'S NOT
ROCKET
SURGERY

it's not
ROCKET
surgery

IT'S
ROC
SU

FEW

ICE IS
FEW

ICE IS
FEW

ICE IS
FEW

A CURFEW

PATIENCE IS
A CURFEW

PATIENCE IS
A CURFEW

PATIENCE IS
A CURFEW

day day day
day day day
day day day
day day day

day

ALL'S ALL'S ALL'S ALL'S
ALL'S ALL'S ALL'S ALL'S
ALL'S ALL'S ALL'S ALL'S
ALL'S ALL'S ALL'S ALL'S
ALL'S ALL'S ALL'S ALL'S
ALL'S ALL'S ALL'S ALL'S
ALL'S ALL'S ALL'S ALL'S
WELL WELL WELL WELL
WELL WELL WELL WELL
WELL WELL WELL WELL
WELL W
WELL W
WELL W

THAT THAT THAT THAT
THAT THAT THAT THAT
THAT THAT THAT THAT
THAT THAT THAT THAT
THAT THAT THAT THAT
THAT THAT THAT THAT
THAT THAT THAT THAT
ENDS ENDS ENDS ENDS
ENDS ENDS ENDS ENDS

half of one,
six dozen
of the other

half of one,
six dozen
of the other

half of one,
six dozen
of the other

half of one,
six dozen
of the other

half of one,
six dozen
of the other.

half of one,
six dozen
of the other

half of one,
six dozen
of the other

half of one,
six dozen
of the other

half of one,
six dozen
of the other

half of one,
six dozen
of the other

half of one,
six dozen
of the other

half of one,
six dozen
of the other

half of one,
six dozen
of the other

half of one,
six dozen
of the other

half of one,
six dozen
of the other

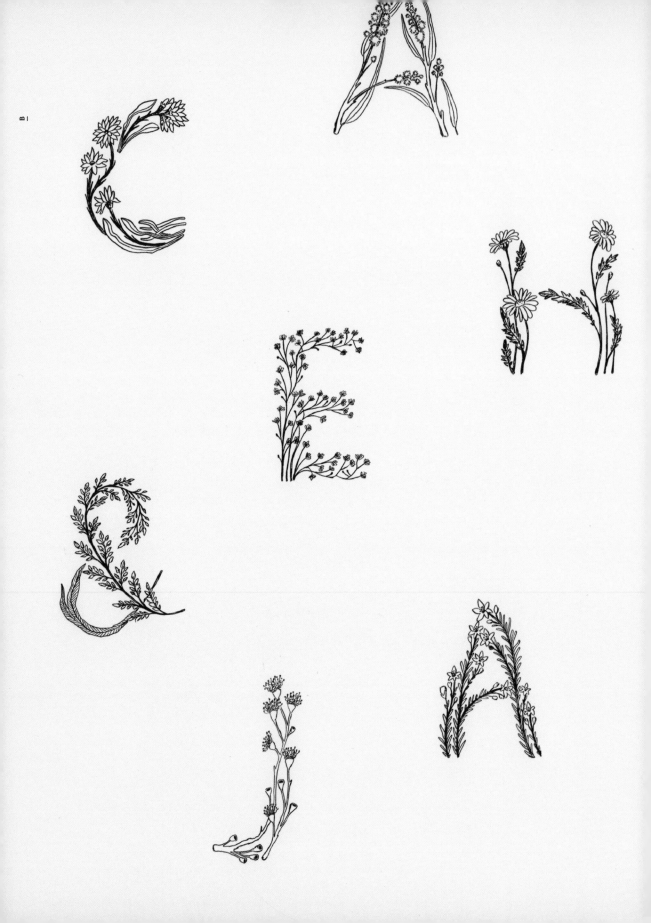

Franco Cervi

Milan · Italy

'Sketching represents a fundamental moment in my creative process,' says Franco Cervi, type designer and founder of 279 Editions, 'because it allows me to build a practically inexhaustible reservoir of ideas and solutions. Drawings must be meaningful, and contain as much information as possible about the project that is taking shape. They are tools at the service of design, so I have never been overly concerned about their "beauty", in the traditional sense of the word.'

Franco's notebooks often look a bit like patchwork quilts, a progressive layering of sketches, made at different times, on various and improvised surfaces: a napkin in a bar, the back of a leaflet, the margin of a newspaper. In such moments, he explains, 'I often find myself drawing with great urgency. Only later are these fragments assembled into organized notebooks, and combined with other diagrams and notes.'

Franco believes that sketches are very personal, even intimate. 'They contain extemporaneous visions and positive design details, as well as mistakes, weaknesses and hesitations,' he explains, 'contrasting features that, when taken together, reveal the substance of every designer.'

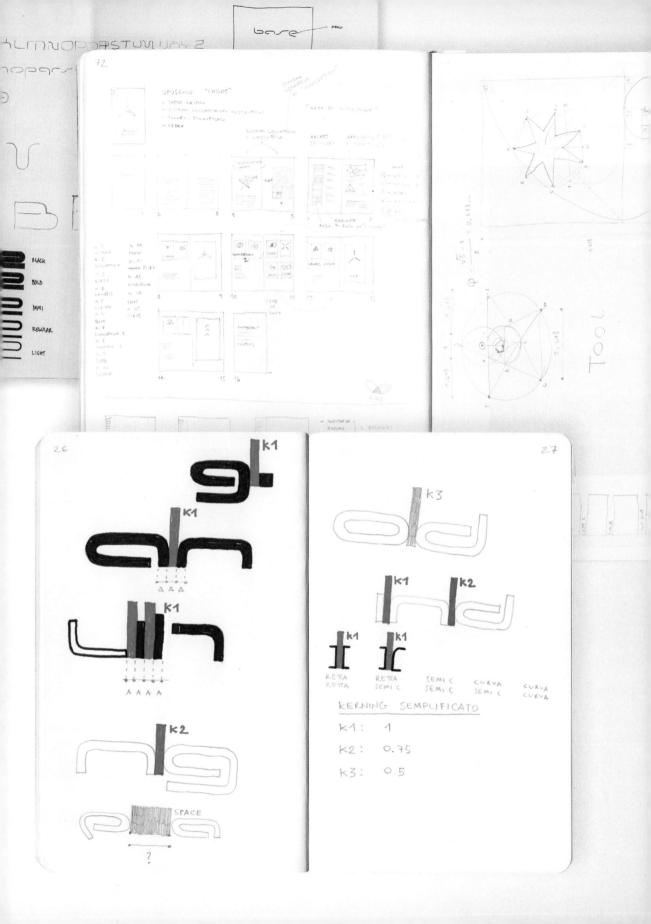

Nadine Chahine
London · UK

'So far my designs have been reliant on computer drawing, with very little manual work,' says Lebanese type designer Nadine Chahine, who works as an Arabic specialist at Monotype. 'But lately I've felt that there is a quality of movement I won't be able to capture without going back to ink and paper.'

It was when Nadine began practising calligraphy with a brush that she finally felt able to explore the concepts of energy, speed and movement in letterforms. This gave her an insight into how the shapes could evolve. 'I would have struggled to find this without sketching,' she explains. 'I'm not yet sure how this will feed into my designs, but I'm looking forward to exploring it!'

Shown here are sketches from Nadine's first week of training with master calligrapher Samir Sayegh. 'I was focusing on traditional Naskh calligraphy, and on the last day decided to switch to a Japanese brush, just to see what I could come up with,' she says. 'These are after only one hour of playing around! It's turned out to be a lot of fun and quite addictive, so I hope to be doing more of this.'

At the moment, Nadine is 'loving' the Japanese rounded brushes. 'Very nice to hold and draw with,' she says. 'I'm still practising calligraphy and drawing on paper for now, but am looking forward to exploring other mediums.'

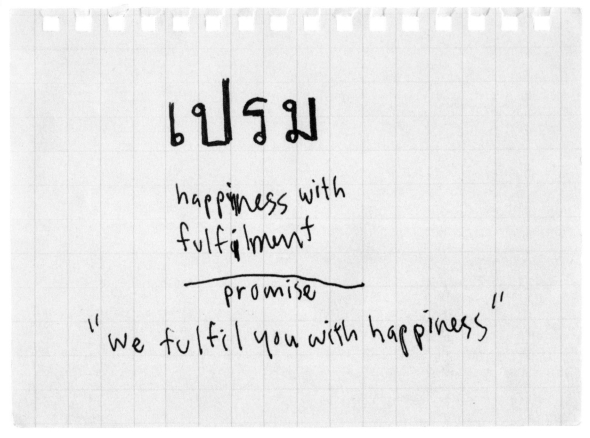

เปรม

happiness with
fulfilment
—————————
promise
" we fulfil you with happiness"

Kritbodee Chaicharoen

New York • New York • USA

Graphic designer Kritbodee Chaicharoen believes that sketching is the most important part of his design process – the first step, in fact, in seeing what the images in his head will look like.

'It takes a very short space of time to translate what I am envisioning into something I can actually see,' he says. 'When I sketch, the result doesn't need to be perfect. Just draw something! Do it fast. I can feel my brain flowing freely when I am sketching.'

These days he tends to use a pen, because, he says, 'the pen makes me feel more confident. With pencils, I can easily erase the marks, which slows down my decision-making. With pens, I don't really care about what is right or wrong. Just put it out there, and learn something.'

With the sketches for Thai lifestyle brand Prem (shown here), Kritbodee remembers thinking that he had nailed it. 'Then I looked at them again, and realized that the final design wasn't what I had intended,' he says. 'I had so many sketches, but the one I liked best was a simple drawing I had made at the start. It is almost the first picture that came to my mind when I took on this project.'

เปรม
PREM

เปรม
PREM

เปรม
PREM

เปรม
PREM

เปรม
PREM

เปรม
PREM

เปรม
PREM

เปรม
PREM

เปรม
PREM

เปรม
PREM

เปรม
PREM

เปรม
PREM

เปรม
PREM

เปรม
PREM

เปรม
PREM

เปรม
PREM

เปรม
PREM

เปรม
PREM

เปรม
PREM

เปรม
PREM

เปรม
PREM

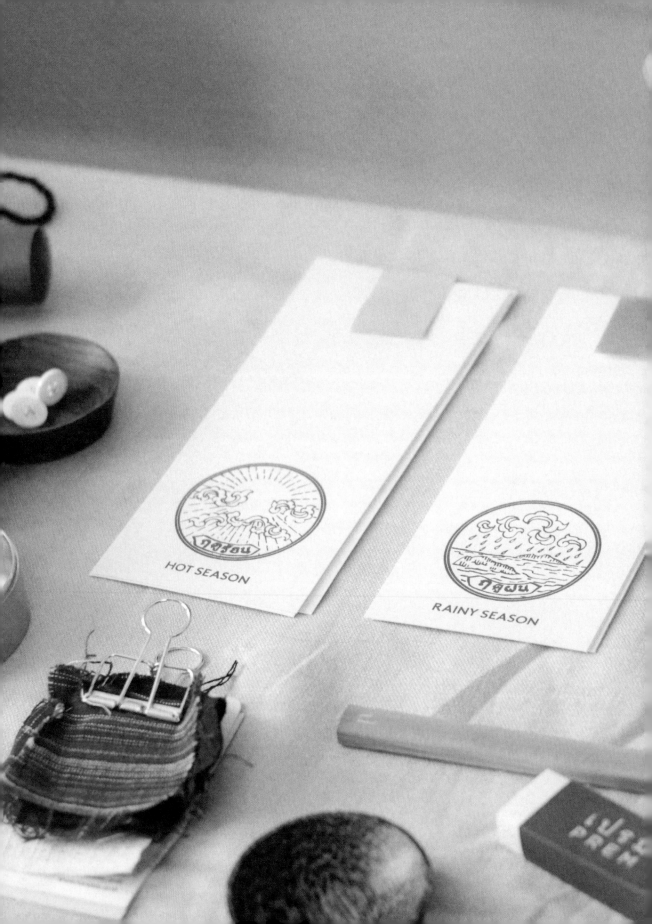

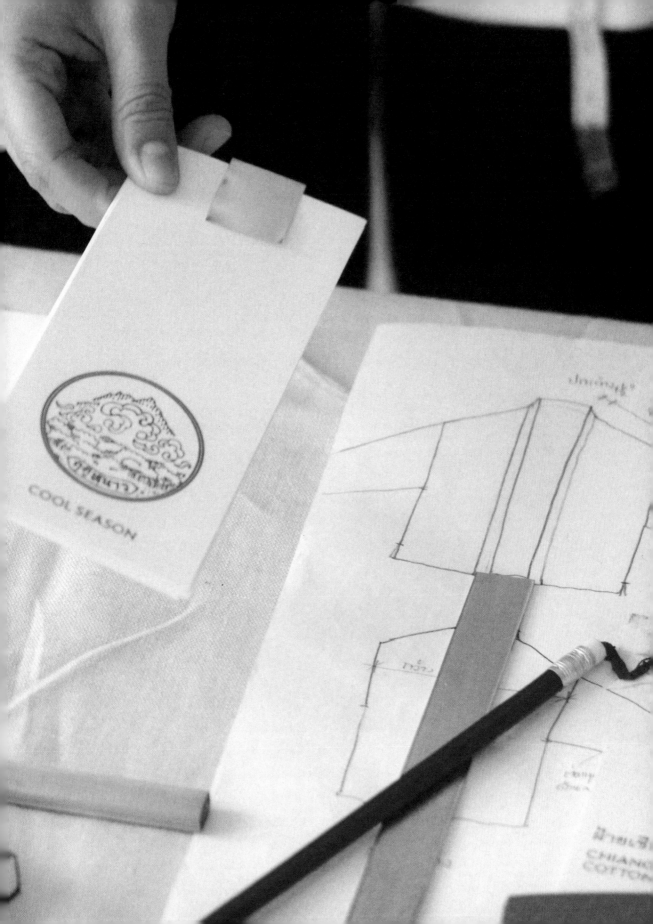

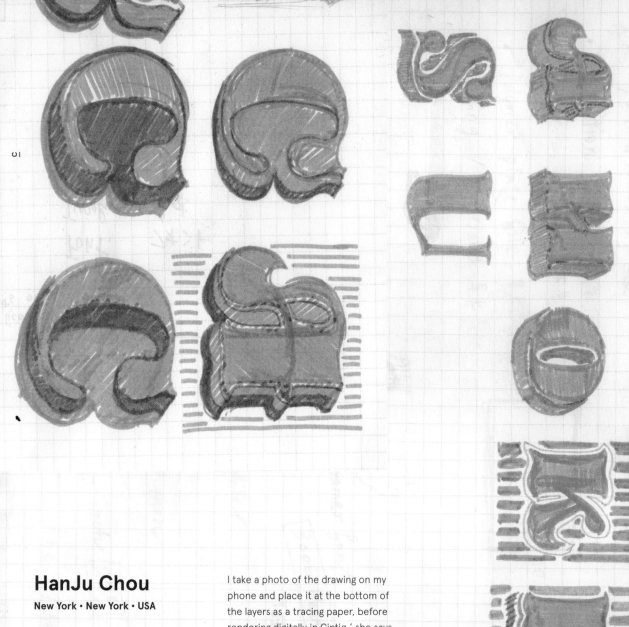

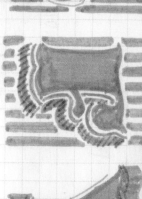

HanJu Chou

New York • New York • USA

'When the beginnings of ideas are floating around in my head, I will do thumbnail sketches to speed up the process,' says motion-graphics designer HanJu Chou. 'Only when my mind is clear will I go directly to the design. To start with, my sketches tend to be quite loose and organic, allowing me to see what forms look most appealing.'

HanJu will produce several pencil sketches to see how many variations will emerge, before tightening one of them. 'If I need to work digitally,

I take a photo of the drawing on my phone and place it at the bottom of the layers as a tracing paper, before rendering digitally in Cintiq,' she says. 'Sketching in Cintiq isn't that different to sketching on paper. It is even easier to erase the strokes with cmd+Z than with an eraser!'

At the moment, HanJu's attentions are taken up by designing a typeface for chromatic wood type. 'By delving into type design,' she explains, 'I began to think more about how the technique (laser engraving) and materials (maple woods) interact with the designs.' For three weeks, she gave herself notes – in both English and Chinese – with feedback for modifications the next day.

1.66 × 9 =

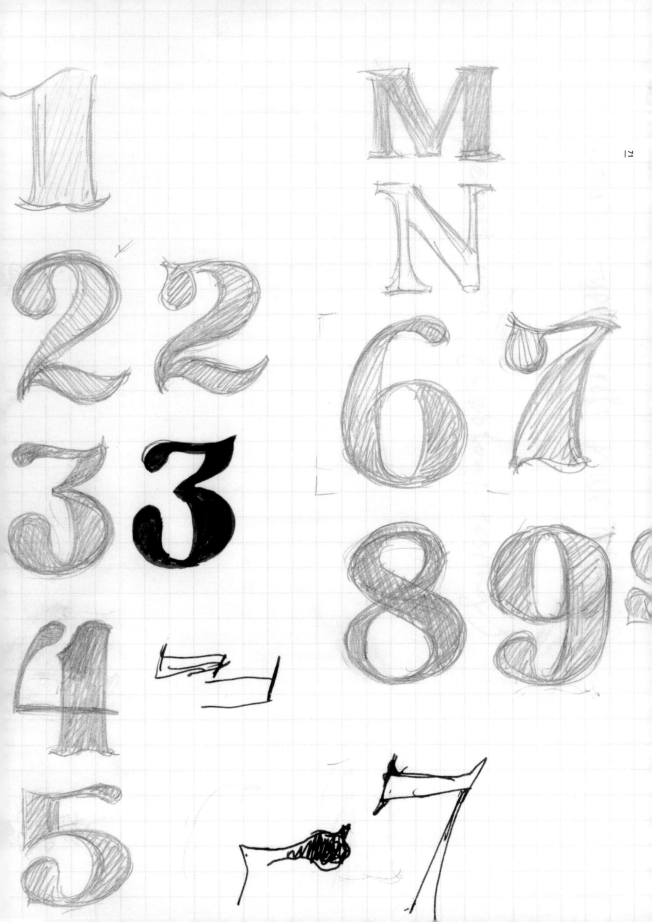

Xavier Dupré

Phnom Penh · Cambodia

French typeface designer Xavier Dupré loves his sketchbooks. 'I always buy more than I can use,' he admits, 'and in the same one might mix live-model drawings, sketches for letterforms or calligraphy, and any number of other projects.'

As 99 per cent of his work is done on the computer screen, sketching is a very small part of Xavier's refining process. The computer's drawing tools are powerful enough, he finds, to discover the correct shape directly with Bézier curves, but sketching helps in formulating new ideas.

'I don't sketch everyday,' he says, 'but occasionally I need to stay away from the computer and enjoy the contact with paper – sometimes to find a shape of a typeface I'm working on, but mostly because I like writing with a calligraphic pen or felt-tip marker (although I might recut the tip). Some studies are redrawn onscreen and become fonts, but many of them stay in the sketchbook.'

Although Xavier admits that the iPad Pro 'seems really great for creating and writing directly onscreen', he uses a 'normal pen to write in a small size, a felt-tip pen for drawing in a larger size and calligraphic pen or felt-tip marker for calligraphy'. He also uses a brush pen for 'lively writing'.

Recently, Xavier wrote down the name of the place where he was drawing as a model. 'It was kind of a bar-and-art gallery called "Show Box",' he explains. 'I rendered it in a personal version of Blackletter, then decided to develop a typeface from the result. Sometimes a quick sketch can be transformed into an interesting typeface.'

ABCDEFG
AYKLMNOPQ
UVWXY
0123456789
KOHTONSA
KRONGK
KAMPUCHEA
ABCDEFGH
MNOPQRSTO
WXYZ DX.

à Khep

Kampot
Cambodia
Tracn

ricanisme

Somelier

Bourgogne

Beaune

Bienne

ABCDE Mauric

BDVVV

Mau
Mau
M
NN
Nan

Veni Vidi Vici

Phnom

yzi Phenh sspi

qui q q

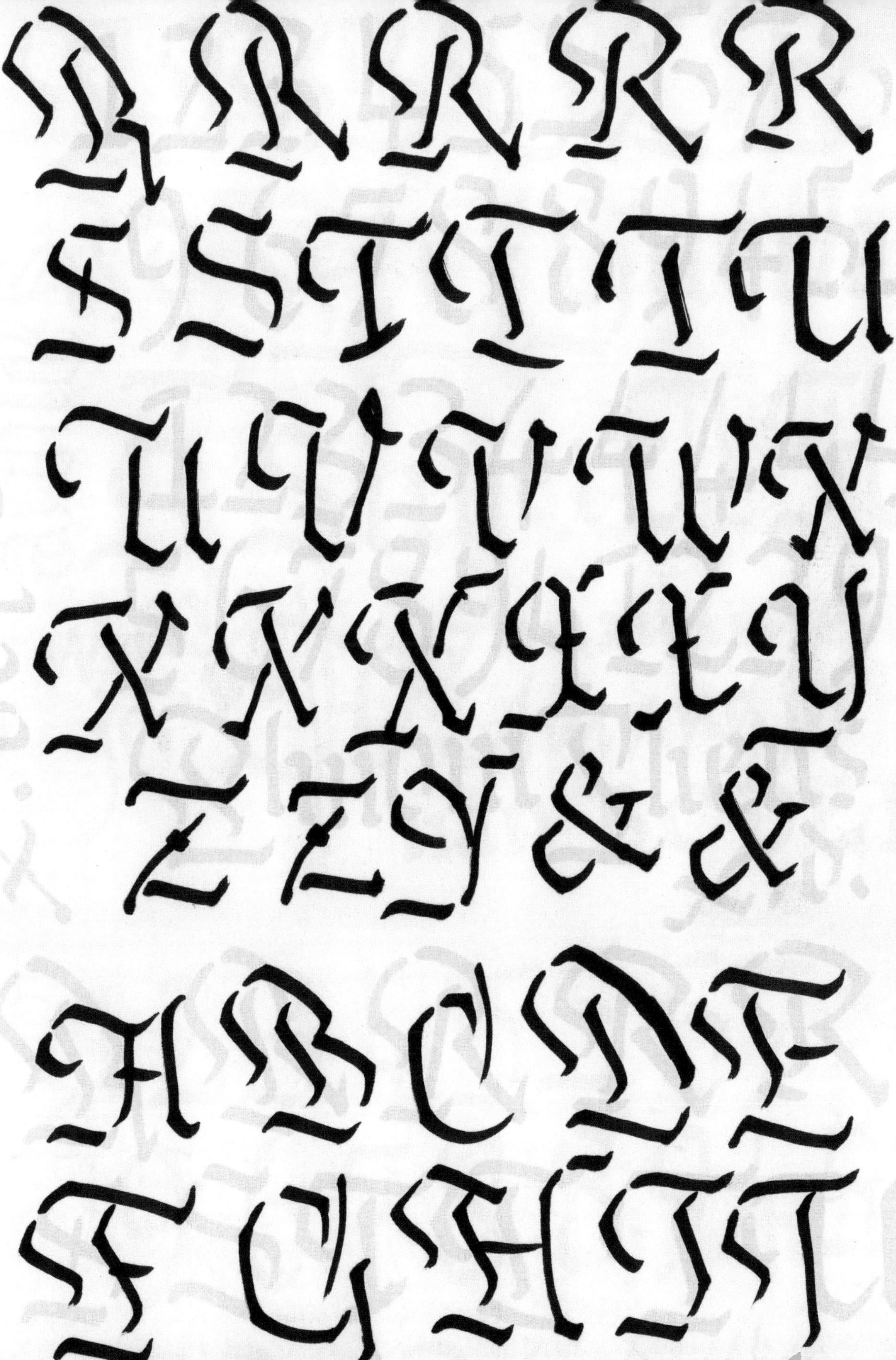

R R R R R R

S S T T T U

U U V V V W X

X X X X X Y

Z Z Y & &

A B C D E

F G H I

an anesilor

aênenaris r

saneh l'aime
alos l'ai
a aen
ao

anesiaygge

anesconsicghjklm

Berlin 2004 Auschwitz - Polen

a a n n Haus ha h

res anacoreteln a d

a ânäcmit acete ane

avaniervomabineriver

a binchia

El Fantasma de Heredia

Buenos Aires · Argentina

'Sketching is absolutely THE WAY WE THINK,' is the bold claim of El Fantasma de Heredia, an experimental group formed in 1992 and co-ordinated by Anabella Salem and Gabriel Mateu. 'It is also often the case that the first sketches or drawings become the finished article,' explains Anabella. 'We redo them, but in general the first is the best, the freshest.'

It is this lack of perfection, the group feels, that gives each sketch its greatest virtue. Pens and pencils are their everyday tools. 'We like brushes, but pens and pencils are faster, and are always in your bag or on the table,' Anabella says. 'When I have a pen in my hand, I never consciously think that whatever I am drawing or writing might be the final result. Quite often I end up scribbling on a piece of paper that already has a drawing on it, because I'm just playing. Then I look at it and think, "This is good! I want to use it and it's on a corner of my son's maths exam!"'

The group's work appears on clean surfaces, white paper of any size – 'but also napkins, when an idea emerges in a bar, for example,' says Anabella. An homage to Pierre Bernard, co-founder of the French design group Grapus, was produced on the day the group learned of his death in 2015. 'We couldn't believe we were writing "Adieu, Pierre",' remembers Anabella. 'Perhaps the saddest sketch we ever did.'

WAW

Wystawa plakatów
el Fantasma de Heredia
Galeria Salon Akademii
— WARSZAWA —

WAW

WYSTAWA PLAKATÓW
el FANTASMA DE HEREDIA
GALERIA SALON AKADE
— WARSZAWA —

WAW

Wistawa Plakatów
el Fantasma de Hered
Galeria Salon Akademi
— WARSZAWA —

WAW

Wystawa plakatów
el Fantasma de H
Galeria Salon Aka
— Warszawa —

Wystawa

Wystaw
el Fanta
Galeria
— W

la FANTASMA de verano 2013

E I

Un Pequeño militante del PO

...arés M. Lobo

con collección relatos
Un Pequeño militante
del PO

Fundar una editorial
es arrojarse al mundo,
al creer que lo que se
hay, de alguna forma,
es necesario que exista.

Pigani
ediciones

Un Pequeño militante del PO

Bahman Eslami

The Hague · Netherlands

When type designer and kinetic graphic designer Bahman Eslami was a teenager in Tehran, he trimmed his reed pen with a sharp knife and ended up losing part of his fingertip. But, he says, it's not for this reason that he considers himself a digital-technology enthusiast who strives to reduce as much manual labour as possible through programming.

'Sketching on paper is an indispensable part of my work,' Bahman insists. 'I love sketching, because it's the fastest way to express my feelings about a letter shape in any given project. The amount of sketching I do depends on the timeline of the project.'

Bahman's first type design was the 'Harir' typeface, which began from sketches. Sketching continued during the digitization of the typeface, producing a huge number of drawings. For the remastering of 'Fedra Arabic', he had to finish the design quickly, so sketching was less on paper and more onscreen. 'The other aspect of this project was that most of the design was done already,' Bahman explains. 'I had to tune it up and finish it for two styles (serif and sans serif) of the Latin family.'

Because Arabic is a cursive wiring system, judging the design is always important, whether it's used in a large section of text or as a single word. 'Sketching could solve the problems I have with particular words when I see the digitized typeface,' Bahman says. 'When I sketch, my hand – somehow magically – draws something that I could never imagine. When I was younger, I was surrounded by drawing and calligraphy. Now when I draw a shape, my hand moves in a way that it cannot when using a mouse or trackpad.'

Bahman used to prefer mechanical pencils, because they move softly across the paper. Recently, however, he has switched his allegiance to marker pens. 'The advantage of markers is their contrast with paper and the fact that the drawing stays fixed for longer,' he explains. 'With pencils, drawings decay when a sheet of paper touches another one. And I wouldn't choose a digital pen for sketching, because of the time gap between moving my hand and the moment lines appear onscreen.'

Bahman prefers paper, because of its physicality. 'I can go to my sketches and turn the pages to see what I've done,' he says, 'but a digital sketch seems ephemeral to me.'

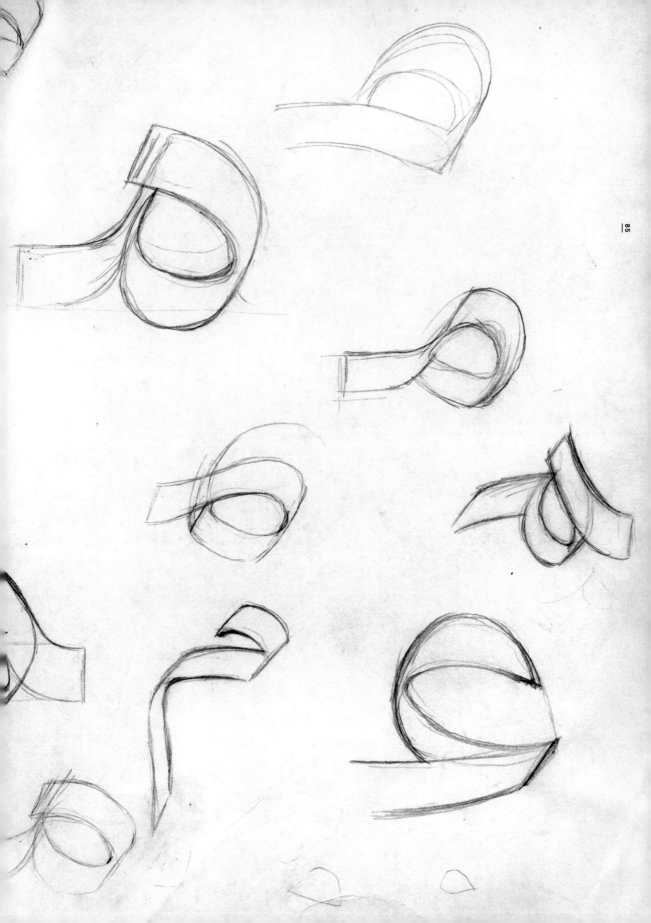

Rarelly to see bucky.
fantom wih Fahr Q

Y COMING SOON h ET &
G ЯК К ky

АІН G aha an

amita Rarely ЮК vernacular

ЯРУСНЫЙ ТЭНГЕ
я olmulefA

ОБ'ЯВЛ Lilienthal Grotesk Gothic

WERASK EN VLAGG

ОЛЕНЬ Ы 1Й

ДРЕВКО

Vera Evstafieva

Cambridge • UK

For type designer, calligrapher and teacher Vera Evstafieva, the sketching process implies a search for the 'best possible direction' for a project. 'It's probably similar to clay modelling in that sense,' she explains. 'Sketching helps in getting closer to a shape or style for a typeface or lettering piece. While sketching, I'm always fascinated by the speed at which a letterform evolves. It's a laborious and wonderful time when an idea emerges.'

Sketching was an important part of Vera's education in her native Moscow, and later on the Type And Media course at the Royal Academy of Art in The Hague. 'I learned a lot about forming letters and searching for a character, proportions and unity of letters, with a pencil, pen or brush.'

The character of letters produced by sketching will usually appear exaggerated when compared to the final letterforms of a typeface, so drawing is a way of making some initial decisions when beginning a project. 'Usually I move on to drawing Bézier shapes very soon after sketching,' Vera explains, 'once I have chosen a design direction and the stylistic relationships between letters.'

Vera's choice of tool is based on the type of letters she is designing. A broad-nib pen would suggest ideas for a humanist sans serif, and pencil would aid in developing the shape.

'I've never designed purely geometric, mechanical letters,' she says, 'so I tend to draw or write a preliminary shape by hand, rather than constructing it on computer. Occasionally, a calligraphy style practised for a long time will suddenly give an idea for a typeface, as happened with my "Amalta" typeface, so practise sheets unintentionally become sketches, and remain interesting on their own.'

нопрст

цчшъы

ЗИКЛПУ
ЬЫЪЭЮЯ

+абвгдеж з

quick quartz judge my vow!

...изъят". Бьём "чуждый" цен хвощ! Эй, жлоб! Где ...
...щ в «шкаф». В чащах юга жил был цитрус... —
...B-ick quiz whangs jumpy veldt fox! Quick w...
...quartz judge my vow!

МИНИСТЕРСТВО
ФИНАНСОВЪ

ДЕПАРТАМЕНТЪ
ТОРГОВЛИ
И
МАНУФАКТУРЪ

Директору Товарищества
Городищенской суконной фабри
ки Четверикова, С. И. Четверико
ву.

Вслѣдствіе поданнаго, сов
мѣстно съ представителями
Товарищества Даниловской
Камвольной Мануфактуры
торговаго и промышленн
товарищества, Владим
...ссъ" и товарищества
...мануфактуръ

Образцы шрифтовъ

Q Q Q R U V V W X
T Time RК ХП T N N
ИКЛямбдаМ НОПР
ТУПКА бфр Ф Рп
ЦЦЩ Бух Югоа

Kolomna Script

Владимир

Мария Гео

Ал Алекса

00 13223

Сергеевич

ргиевна В

ндр ИйЙ

5124 67839

Oded Ezer

Tel Aviv • Israel

After sketching an idea for a typeface, typographic artist Oded Ezer allows himself to 'forget' the idea without losing it altogether, thus, he says, 'making room in my head for the next one'.

Shown here are sketches and ideas for several new sans-serif, half-serif and serif Hebrew fonts, from Oded's 'Glyphs' application. The experiments with different materials and techniques (overleaf) were later used for Jonathan Safran Foer's *New American Haggadah* (2012). Rather than simply following traditional calligraphic and typographic techniques, Oded chose to develop a different one every one or two spreads, to give the book a more contemporary, even radical, look and feel.

The experiments and ideas on pp. 94–5 were later used in eight short typographic videos created for the *Memory Palace* exhibition at the Victoria and Albert Museum in London in 2013. The exhibition presented novelist and journalist Hari Kunzru's graphic novella, as interpreted by 20 graphic artists, creating an immersive environment for this dystopian work of fiction.

'Instead of making a two-dimensional printed work, I thought it would be more powerful to show me eating the letters, burning them, and so on,' Oded explains. 'It was a way of interpreting this unique story.'

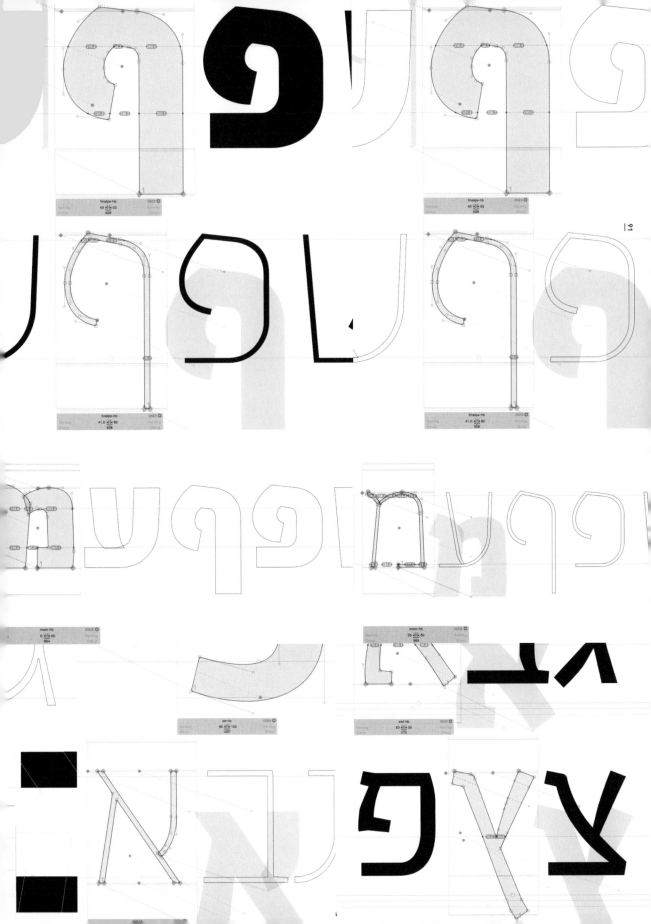

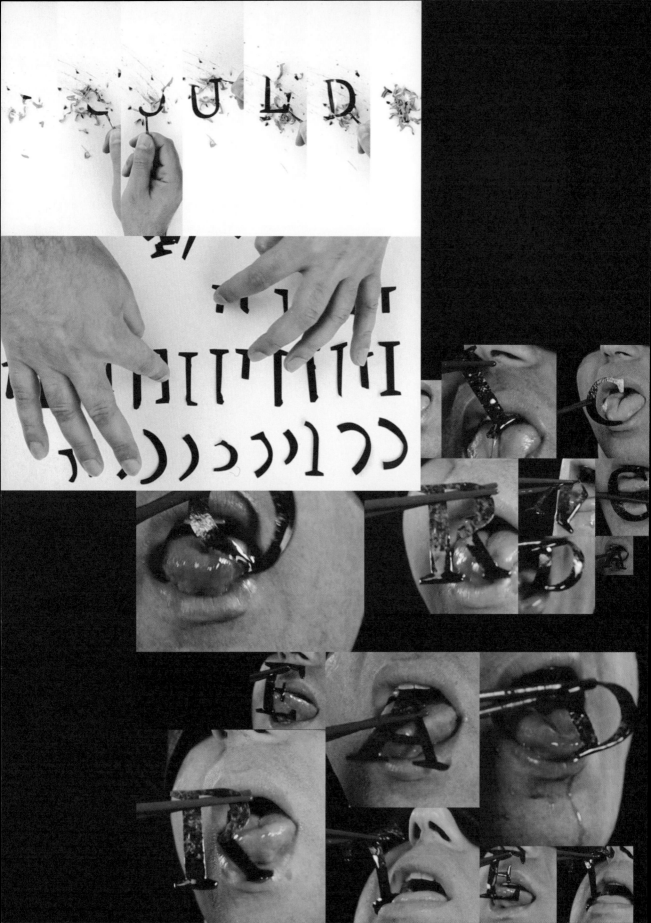

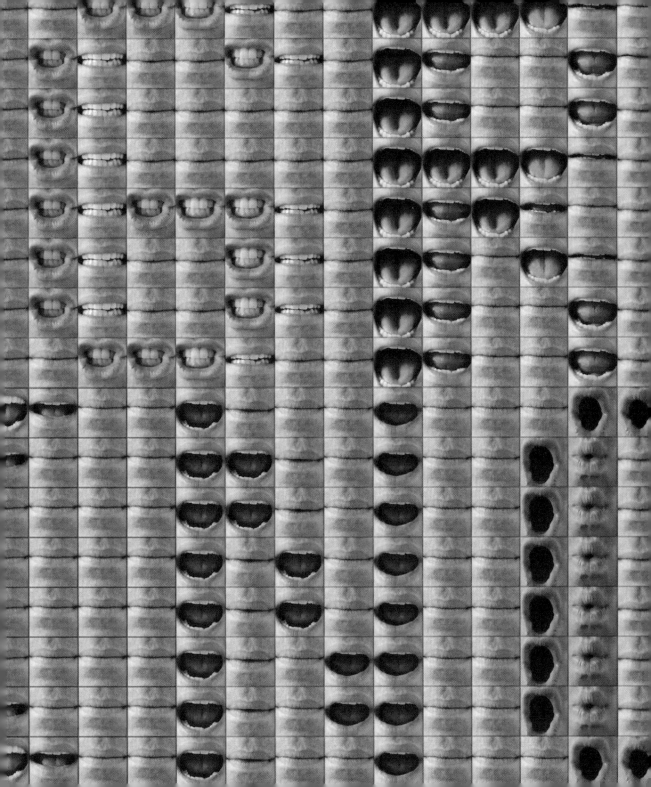

Pablo Ferro

Los Angeles • California • USA

The frightening absurdity of the biting Cold War satire that is Stanley Kubrick's *Dr Strangelove or: How I Learned to Stop Worrying and Love the Bomb* (1964) was established from the first frame of the hand-scrawled main title sequence, designed by Pablo Ferro. The film's title sequence, with its deliberately crude graffiti-like scrawls of hand-drawn letters was unlike anything that had come before. The whole thing, one could argue, was a sketch in the raw.

Having cut his teeth in the comic-book industry, Cuban-born Pablo was among the first designers to create hand-drawn animated commercials. He had directed and edited scores of these early television commercials, each a mini-experimental film, and was known for his innovative technique of using a kinetic quick-cut method for editing a montage of static images (engravings, photographs and pen-and-ink drawings) presented in motion and with sound.

In the 1950s, most commercials were shot with one or two stationary cameras, but Pablo took full advantage of stop-motion technology, and shot his jerky footage with a handheld Bolex. Unlike his contemporaries, he loved typography, and introduced type in motion on the television screen, showing a preference for Victorian decorative display faces (which later evolved into more contemporary fonts). Everything he did began as a drawing, rather than a metal piece of type, or a photograph of one.

Pablo's rapid-fire cinematic editing style also helped define filmmaking in the following decade. He was known to cut scenes into multiple frames that played simultaneously, as if they were collages from a sketchbook.

For anyone glued to the television in the mid-1960s, the most exciting animation on air was the fast-paced kinetic TV logo for Burlington Mills, for which Pablo animated the stitching of a square as a staccato musical rhythm. Now in his eighties, his sketches continue to exude the energy that is packed into his designs.

F1

89

40

Cashew Peanut Almond Pecan Macadamia Pistachio nut Hazel acorn Walnut

Njoki Gitahi

New York • New York • USA

Each project begins with a sketch of some sort, notes graphic designer Njoki Gitahi, whether it's a five-second rough drawing or a fully detailed 3D view. Either way, sketching gives her the means to quickly shake out all the bad ideas, and to begin developing and improving those with potential.

'Initial sketches can capture a spirit that can get lost once you smooth everything out digitally,' she explains. 'Referring back to the sketch is a good way of making sure the final work is as robust as what I began with.' This process causes her to reflect on psychologist Mihaly Csikszentmihalyi's notion of flow: 'I can zone out for quite a while once I start putting pen to paper. I find the immediacy of thinking and making at the same time quite satisfying.'

Njoki's routine is to begin with a pencil or pen for very early, open exploration. 'For times when I already have a pretty well-formed concept that I want to iterate quickly, I jump onto the computer, especially if it involves geometric shapes and precise proportions,' she explains. 'That way I'm not distracted by the misshapen circles I always seem to draw, and can quickly add in colour or stroke variations.'

Any paper scrap will do, but Njoki hates the idea of losing a stray sketch. 'I usually either draw in a notebook or tape scraps of sketches into one later. I like making my own notebooks out of trimmed sketchpads that I perfect-bind so that they lay flat easily.'

G|

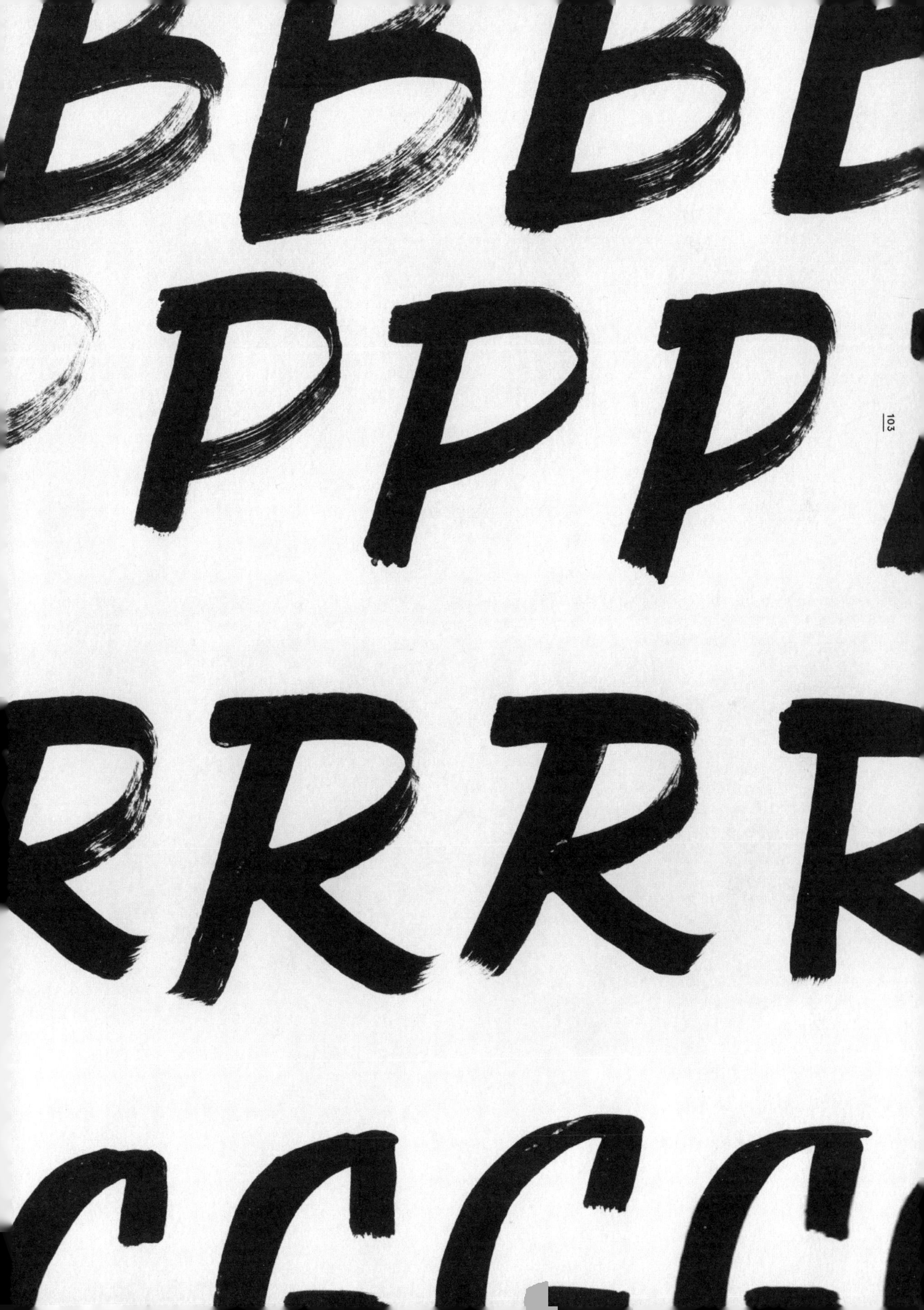

abcdefghijklmnopqrstuvwxyz

abcdefghijklmnopqrstuvwxyz

abcdefghijklmn
opqrstuvwxyz

abcdefghijklmnopqrstuvwxyz

ABCDEFGHIJKLMNOPQRST
UVWXYZ

ABCDEFGHIJKLMNOPQRSTUVWXYZ
ABCDEFGHIJKLMNOPQRS
TUVWXYZ

ABCDEFGHIJKLMNOPQR
STUVWXYZ

ABCDEFGHIJKLMNOPQRSTUVWXYZ
abcdefghijklmnopqrstuv
wxyz

ABCDEFGHIJKLMNOPQR
STUVWXYZ

ABCDEFGHIJKLMNOPQ
RSTUVWXYZ

ART LOVE TIME & MONEY

Milton Glaser

New York · New York · USA

'A real question for many of us, if we have an artistic vision,' says legendary graphic designer Milton Glaser, 'is how to reconcile our sense of artistry and the pleasure we get from making things with the demands of a business that very often is not interested in that. So the advice I would give somebody is to think in the long run, because if you have a long career – spanning 30, 40, 50 years – you have to think of what will sustain you and keep you interested for that length of time.'

Now in his ninth decade, Milton is an inveterate picture-maker. Wherever he is, with whatever tool he is holding, he can be found sketching ideas, images, visual thoughts. Every aspect of the process is about finding the clearest communications solution, he says.

'One of the great problems of being a designer is that you find yourself increasingly narrowed, doing more and more specialized things that you've done a hundred times before,' he continues.

'For me, the way out was to broaden the canvas, to try to do things that I was not very experienced at doing, to develop a range of activities, so that I couldn't be forced into a corner and left to dry. While that is not the solution for everyone, that is a consideration people must at least examine before they embark on a course, for once they have mastered the professional requirement, it may no longer hold any interest for them.'

FLY
THE
THON

PINK

MAHALIA JACKSON
EASTER SUNDAY
PHILHARMONIC HALL
LINCOLN CENTER

Sunday, March 26, 1967 4:30 & 8:30 P.M.
TICKETS: 5.50, 5.00, 4.50, 4.00,
3.50, 2.95 Tickets Available at:
Lincoln Center Box Office &
Bloomingdales TR 4-2424

TINT OF

TINT

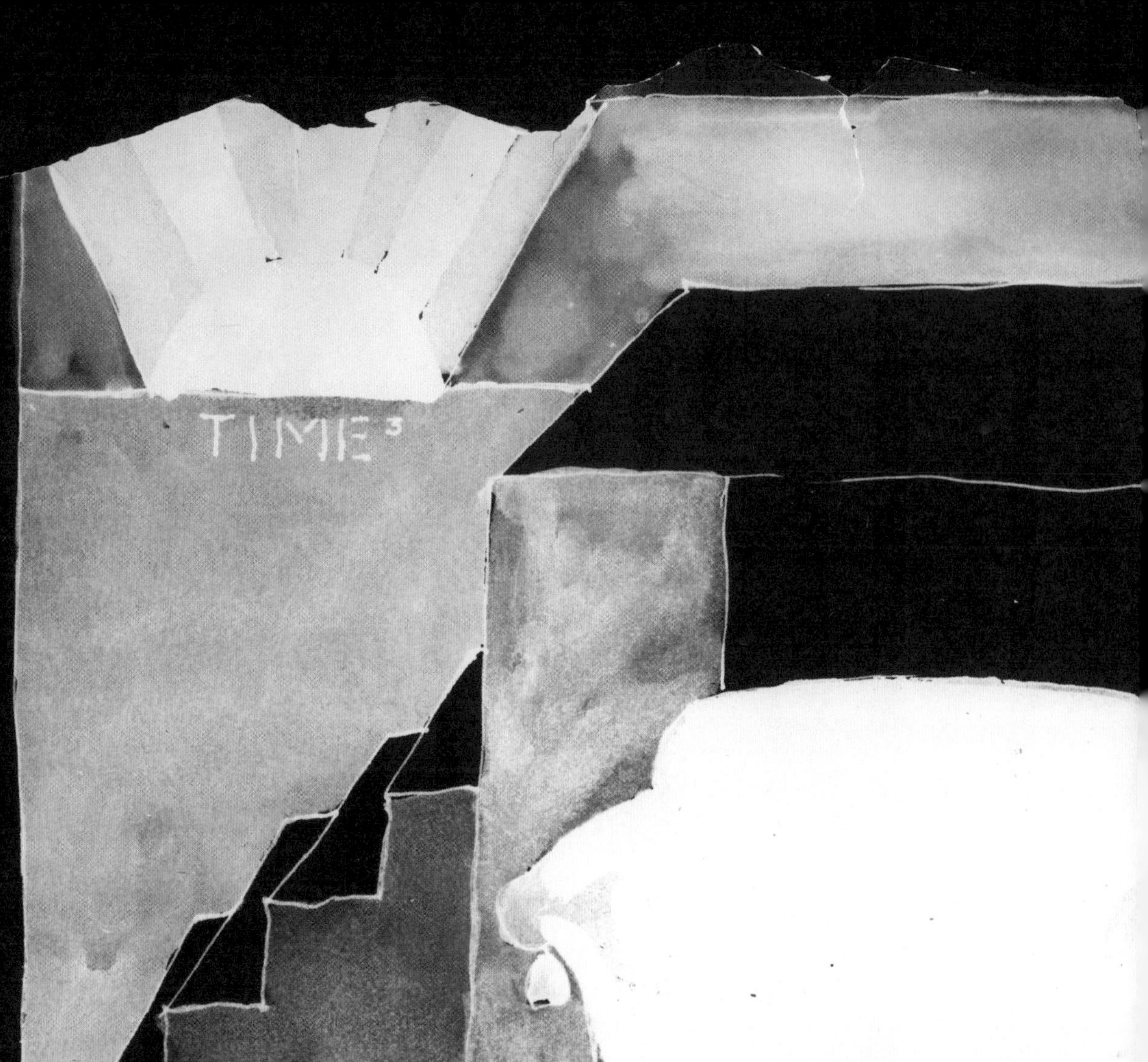
TIME³
ART¹
LOVE²
ART¹ LOVE² TIME³ & MONEY

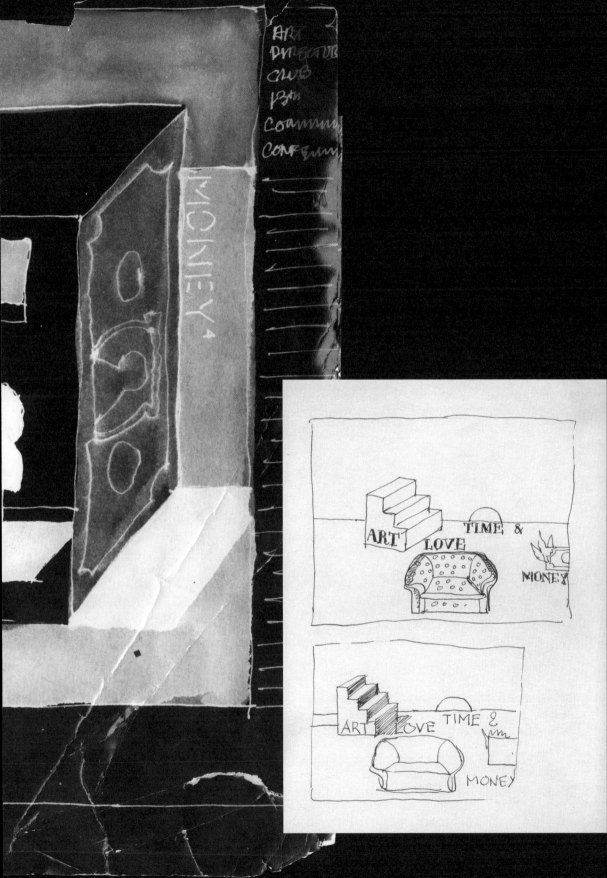

Baruch Gorkin

Brooklyn • New York • USA

Sketching is an essential part of Baruch Gorkin's design process, especially at the inception stages. He does most of his drawings in fountain pen-friendly sketchbooks or on tracing paper, when he uses a pencil. 'At times I will make a fairly tight pencil rendition of a letterform,' he says, 'but that, typically, is when I feel lost trying to refine the letter digitally and need a fresh direction. Other than that, I do all the refinement and finishing work digitally.'

What appeals to Baruch most about the design process is the fluidity, immediacy and distance, the 'ability to see whether a particular visual idea "has legs", which should be evident without doing any letterform refinement'. He tends to view the computer as a tool for developing the letterform, refining it and producing variations, even when the final result represents a huge departure from the original sketch. He explains that the process 'differs from sketching in the most essential way, because real sketching is where new ideas are born'.

Baruch notes that his favourite sketches, and indeed letters, involve a Hebrew semi-cursive typeface (Rashi) that has evolved to such an extent it is now difficult to recognize its original calligraphic structure and connection to the 'square' Hebrew.

'I really wanted my design for "Venecia Hebrew" to be imbued with those qualities,' he says. 'My calligraphic studies of these letterforms were done not so much as sketches for the typeface, but rather as a way to discover their underlying calligraphic makeup and trace their evolutionary process.'

ממקזזהפ

זסוזו ב בא
צל קטיך דגדהז
לח ל ג ת
ח חו וח
טי שף ף יכככ
ח ב ד ד ה זק

מנס
קרתשטי
ע צדק
חב ג ד ל
טי ד ל מ מ רשת
ז ע
חבגד הווח חז
גו
זח
חבג
ח
חבגד

מ ח ל צ ש א
הזי ד ז צ ב ל
רב י ט ו

ח 3 ז ר
להווזח
ט פף

ט ח ז

Giuseppe Del Greco

Milan · Italy

Ever since he was a child, designer Giuseppe Del Greco has been fervently sketching. 'I always have pen and paper with me,' he explains. 'When I was at school, I was the only one who made drawings the teachers praised.'

Sketching for Giuseppe is the first understanding of a problem. It is also, he says, 'a strictly selfish activity that gives me real and personal pleasure, and a curious feeling of being powerful'. He refers to 'real' sketching as the point at which the mind meets the hand, where together they generate shapes, relationships and meanings. 'But when a precise mental sketch has already been done,' he concedes, 'you can work directly on the computer.'

Giuseppe draws primarily on loose paper and in sketchbooks, as well as on the backs of envelopes and receipts. 'Sometimes I like to let sketches grow,' he says, 'like a parasite plant in the blank spaces of a piece of paper.'

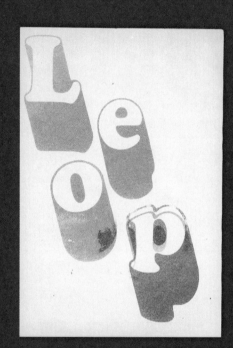

All YO CAN EAT

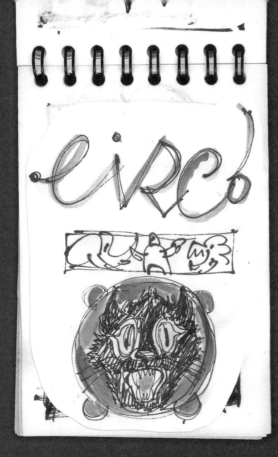

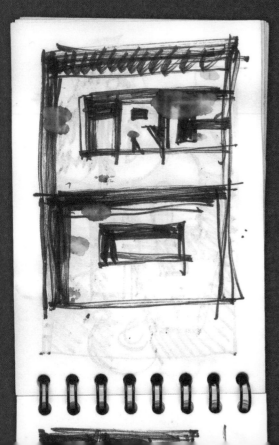

Viktor Hachmang

The Hague · Netherlands

The act of sketching is an essential part of illustrator Viktor Hachmang's daily routine. Each illustration he creates starts out in a sketchbook, either in the form of a thumbnail sketch or as a short note-to-self.

'Sketches are the foundation on which I build my finished work,' he says.

'Most of the time, the sketch serves as an underdrawing, refining linework in light- to gradually darker-coloured pencils, for example, or tracing a sketch to end up with a final line drawing. On some occasions, however, I have spent hours trying to retain a certain mood or elegance in the final lines, which I managed to capture almost instantly with a simple sketch.'

To get into his creative flow, Viktor uses an ordinary pencil, because he enjoys the feeling of graphite on paper, as well as the wide range of effects and

textures that can be achieved with a simple grey lead and the ease in altering the design afterwards. Viktor views sketching as a 'harmless' act, in the sense that there are no rules or wrong way to go about it.

'It's like thinking out loud,' he says. 'No filter! This can be scary, of course, but I hope that following certain trains of thought can help me to reach a deeper understanding or, at the very least, an interesting point of view.'

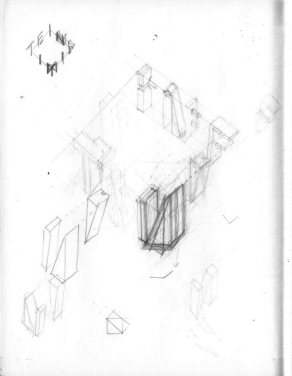

TE I N S I M I

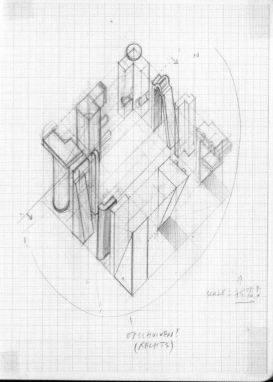

SCALE: 1:5 ½?

OPSCHUIVEN!
(RECHTS)

THE SOUND OF YOUNG HOLLAND

THE SOUND OF YOUNG HOLLAND

T
+HE
SO

THE SOUND OF YOUNG HOLLAND

THE SOUND OF YOUNG HOLLAND

JANUARY 14·15

Dirk Hagner

**San Juan Capistrano
California · USA**

For printmaking artist Dirk Hagner, sketching is an essential part of his work routine, particularly for projects that involve images. When it comes to type, he uses letterpress for developing and experimenting with typographic ideas. 'It is crucial,' he explains, 'because it gives me unfinished results – work that is open to change, accidents – and lets me change direction. It forces me to focus my approach on the essential.'

Dirk's favourite sketching tools 'are definitely brush first, followed by ink pen, and then pencil. To mimic these on the computer seems pointless,' he continues. 'What the computer does is too slick, too intimidating with its clean, "finished" look. It cuts out much of the exploration. For type, I start out with some fonts or writing and doodle with it on the letterpress.'

More formal sketchbooks are rarely used. As Dirk explains, 'most of the time I work on sheets of paper, of all kinds'. He will admit to occasionally liking his letterpress doodles better than the finished article, because of their uninhibited feel, and because 'many new project ideas seem to spring from trying to work out the previous one'.

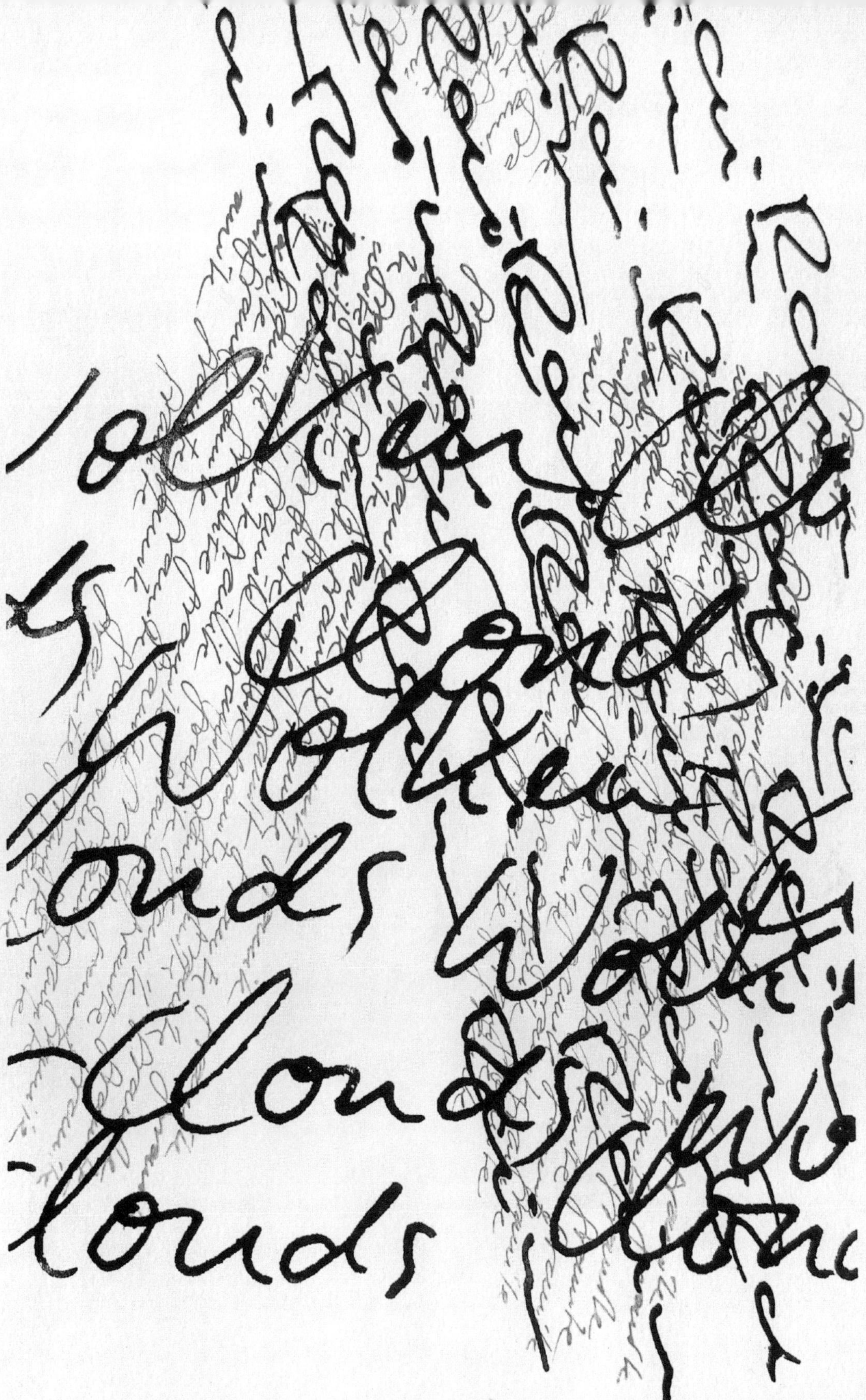
clouds

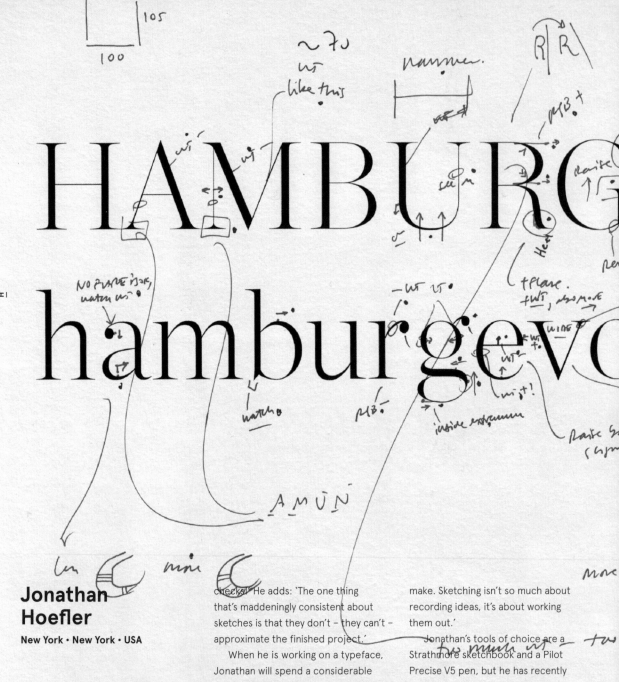

HAMBURG
hamburgevo

Jonathan Hoefler

New York • New York • USA

'I can't think of the last thing I designed
that didn't begin with a sketch,' says
type-design veteran Jonathan Hoefler
of H&Co. 'I always carry a notebook,
and most of the typefaces I design begin
with sketches of one kind or another.'

Jonathan tries to be disciplined
about where he jots his drawings down:
'You have no idea how many ideas
started out on the back of restaurant

checks.' He adds: 'The one thing
that's maddeningly consistent about
sketches is that they don't – they can't –
approximate the finished project.'

When he is working on a typeface,
Jonathan will spend a considerable
amount of time with his sketchbook
(or, more often nowadays, his iPad)
to get the basic ideas down, but
these are impossible to translate
into actual typefaces.

As far as he is concerned, however,
'it's an invaluable way to start a project.
I can't imagine the paralysis of facing
a blank computer screen without
having visualized what I'm going to

make. Sketching isn't so much about
recording ideas, it's about working
them out.'

Jonathan's tools of choice are a
Strathmore sketchbook and a Pilot
Precise V5 pen, but he has recently
bought an iPad Pro with an Apple
Pencil, which, he says, have changed his
life. 'I've doodled with every generation
of artificial pen since the Apple II with
its attached graphics tablet came
out in the 1970s, and this is the first
one that actually feels like a pen. That
my sketches can suddenly be edited,
resized, recoloured, copied and pasted
makes it even more satisfying.'

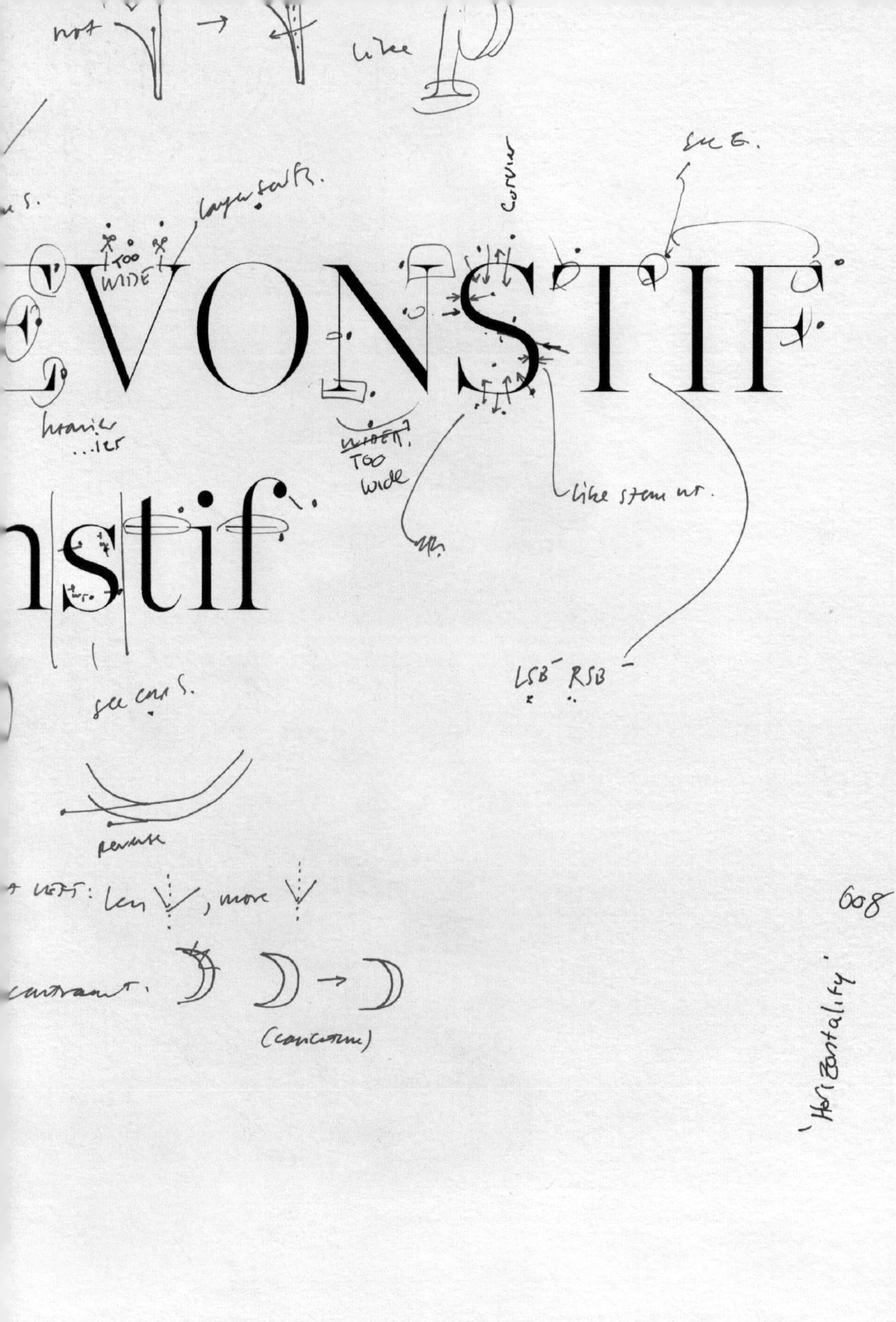

not → like

us.

layer staff.

too wide

EVONSTIF

heavier ...ier

WIDER?
TOO
WIDE

nstif

see cas.

curving

see 6.

like stem wt.

LSB RSB

129

608

see cas.

reverse

LEFT: less, more

contrast.))→)

(concave)

'Horizontality.'

1) I.C. ⊘

2) a, d, g, q.

[START HERE]

I think it's possible that the adjustments we made between the DISP I and ~~DISP XL~~ FIVE I, in letters like "a" —

a → a "rah!"

— might be working against us in this vision. It feels like the a is too oblique, which might be a function of weight missing here:

a

in notes so far are:
"a" — should be less oblique
"d" — should be wider
"g" and "q" — like d, perhaps less so

AND YET, the "p" looks really nice, and it has some these compensations, too.

maybe the a, d, g, q went too far?
TAKE A LOOK AT THESE, p. w/[?] the ___ i.e. b & q p.

Thanks! ✓SS

Form too oblique:
see "nnanonsaoo", but also all letter-specific proofs intensive.

stem needs more straightening than bowl, but both do to some extent.

form can...

slight; and ✓(-) ut through thereas well, from inside!

fghij

131

...ow
...ith b –
...adanese"
...- intensive
...age 1, under "a"

nb: ascenders are all too short, see roman! ✓SS

fghij

wrong dot ✓SS

✓V

✓SS

see d ✓SS
too upright?

...um

...ight need to become more oblique)
but is so it's VERY SUBTLE. Want to run some proofs designed to reveal this?
(nnfnn, nnfnn, ll f ll, ex).

fghij

John Holmstrom

New York • New York • USA

John Holmstrom, co-founder, editor and designer of the legendary and entirely hand-lettered *Punk* magazine, does not ordinarily create lettering designs in his sketchbooks. 'I usually scribble script ideas for comic strips and other nonsense,' he says. 'I use spiral notebooks for ideas, since that is what I scribbled into during high school, and I like the feeling of not working on my schoolwork and goofing off in class.'

John recalls making sketches for the film *CBGB* (2013) after watching an early screening. He takes up the story: 'I went upstairs to the film studio's guest room and knocked out several finished drawings for them. When I got back to New York, Hurricane Sandy had knocked out the power so I wasn't able to deliver all the lettering. What I enjoyed most about working on the film was this "knock-it-out, just-do-it" attitude, which was very punk rock.'

The 'Punk Alphabet' was created for a Japanese clothing company using the *Punk* magazine-logo style. The company had asked for a standard alphabet, but instead John created the logos one by one, drawing on a library of letters, and then using Photoshop to 'warp' them into place. 'To this day, I get requests to hand-letter something for someone, whether it's a book or an article of clothing, whatever,' he explains. 'And I get paid most of the time. So maybe it's for the best that I never made a font of my hand-lettering.'

BRANDO ·· RAMONES ·· GIRLS ·· LEGS

PUNK

NUMBER **1**

JAN.

50¢

HOLMSTROM

LOU REED

Indian Type Foundry

Ahmedabad • India

'When dealing with Indian scripts,' explains Satya Rajpurohit, co-founder of the Indian Type Foundry collective, based in Ahmedabad, 'it is essential to sketch at the beginning of the design process – for form, of course, but mainly to understand the relationship the letters share with their accents and conjuncts.'

He continues: 'As a beginner, it was essential to practise calligraphy, especially for Indic scripts, because each person in the office works on many different scripts at a time and each one has a different angle of stress and stroke modulation. It is useful to sketch during the design process to understand the logic of the typeface, but once a designer gains more experience, then it becomes more of a pleasure. With sketching there are no inhibitions. One is truly free.'

Sketching on any clean surface is enough, he explains. 'We have a large blackboard wall in the office on which we draw, all the time. One member of our group used to be a regular at a local pizza place, where he would draw letters on the receipts and napkins while waiting for his order. Unknown to him, the restaurant had collected his drawings over the years, and presented him with a scrapbook compiled from every one of his sketches.'

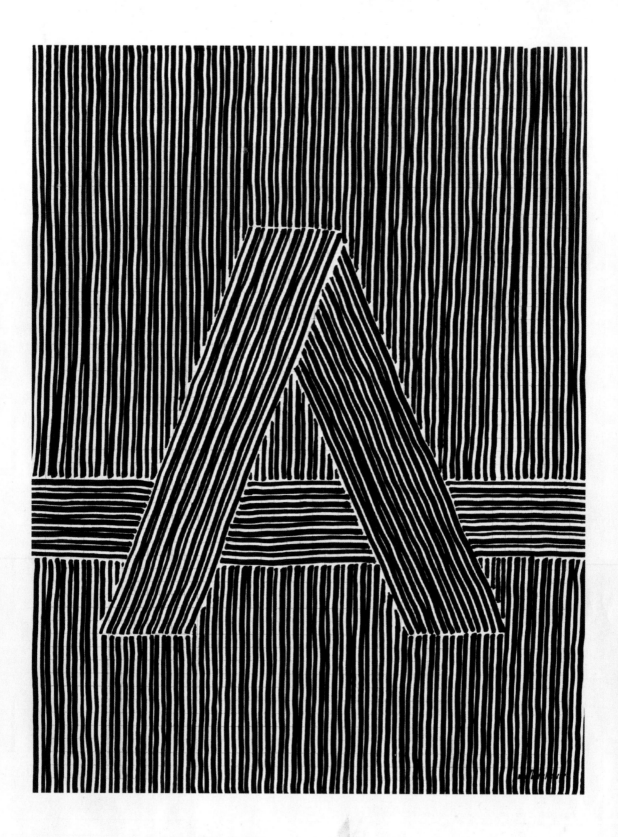

Yanek Iontef

Tel Aviv • Israel

Type designer Yanek Iontef, a specialist in corporate identity and editorial design, also has his own type foundry, Fontef.com. His research centres primarily around the classical Hebrew letter, but he also studies stencil type, particularly how to detach parts of a letter without compromising legibility.

His favourite type design is 'Hadassah', designed by Henri Friedlaender in 1958.

Yanek sketches each time he puts ideas into visual form, before touching a mouse. 'I prefer to take a pencil or pen and piece of paper,' he says. 'While I'm on the phone in the studio, there is always a notebook and pen in front of me. It helps me to concentrate.'

The most satisfying part of sketching, he says, is 'being able to be completely focused on what you are doing, whether a single shape of a character or the whole family, and make improvements

and changes that will make the typeface better. In the end, the users of that typeface will be able to sense that you put so much energy into it.'

About sketching, he adds: 'If there is something very special captured in the hand-drawn line on paper, something I cannot transfer through my eyes and hand holding the mouse, then I scan the sketch to make use of it as a reference tool.'

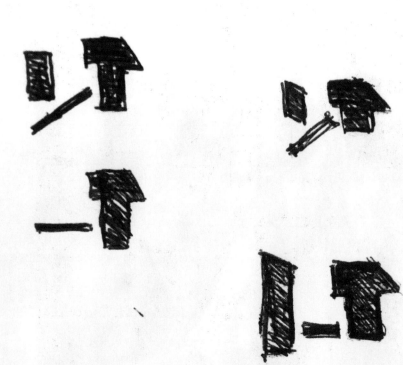

Damoon
Khanjanzadeh

Tehran • Iran

Visual artist and graphic designer
Damoon Khanjanzadeh believes that
'all creatures – plants, humans, trees,
animals – inspire us to create brilliant
design. When I'm designing, I gather
together all of my inspirational things,
alongside my sketches. Sketches live
forever,' he concludes. 'They are the
plan of my design.'

It is no surprise, therefore, that
Damoon is equally reverential about
his type design. He maintains separate
notebooks for each project, because,
as he says, 'sketches are the story of
my typeface design'. About his tools,
he adds: 'I like using pencils during the
sketching process, especially old and
broken pencils. I respect them.'

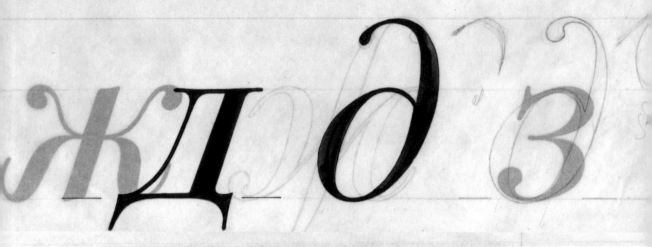

Dmitry Kirsanov

Moscow • Russia

As a graphic designer specializing in website and logo design, Dmitry Kirsanov does not feel that sketching is an essential part of his work routine. He will concede, however, that it 'often helps'. He adds: 'Sketching helps me to better understand and identify a problem. Sketches rarely coincide with the end result, but contribute to realizing it.'

The best part about making sketches, he says, is to 'think with a pencil in hand and have fun with the process'. At first he used all tools equally, but lately he has focused on felt-tip pens and the computer. 'I will draw sketches on any sheet of blank paper, rather than in a sketchbook,' Dmitry explains. He also notes that each drawing is a separate story, but as there are so many, the work will speak for itself.

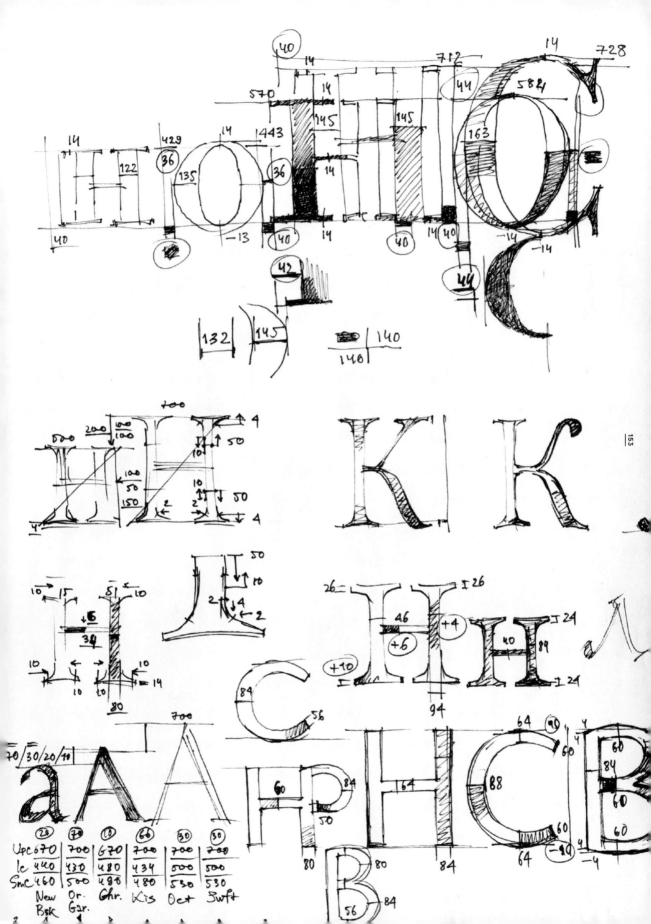

Унцеръ Лютара   Имгеро Ревильони

Бодони   Bodoni

XIX век.

б г д к л м п

Л   Ж ж м ф

П = Bd. + Akad.

↑ Терцизо курсив 1788 ↑ Академ.

Бодони + Академ.   Бодони

б д Д Д Ж Ж

з А А А Ж ж

м М м Ж

В

Sylvia (Di) Kong

Beijing • China

'I sketch all the time,' says Sylvia Kong (also known by her Mandarin name, 'Di'). Preferring to use Muji sketchbooks, with dots or grids on the pages, she works from the beginning to the end of each project and uses the notebook to capture 'some instant inspirations'.

Sylvia creates most of her work in digital format, and looks at her iMac all day long. 'The sketching process makes me think more,' she says. 'The more I draw, the more I gain in confidence. It also pulls me away from the crazy, distracting digital world. I believe sketching is the best way to transform ideas into real designs, and to map my thought and creative process.'

When Sylvia created a type logo for Bailment Café in Xi'an, the ancient capital of China, she went to see the terracotta army of Qin Shi Huang in the morning. 'When I returned to the hotel, I was thinking about using the warriors' faces as a logo for a tradition-fusion dance club,' she explains. 'I struggled, and after an hour it still wasn't working.'

The sketches of the warriors' features 'somehow triggered in my mind the idea for the Bailment Café type logo. And then all of these great type ideas came to me in 5 minutes,' she adds. 'It's the first type logo I made, and it went very well. One year later, the Bailment Café opened another location in Beijing.'

初温下毛通

后笑覆寸都

午的线一此

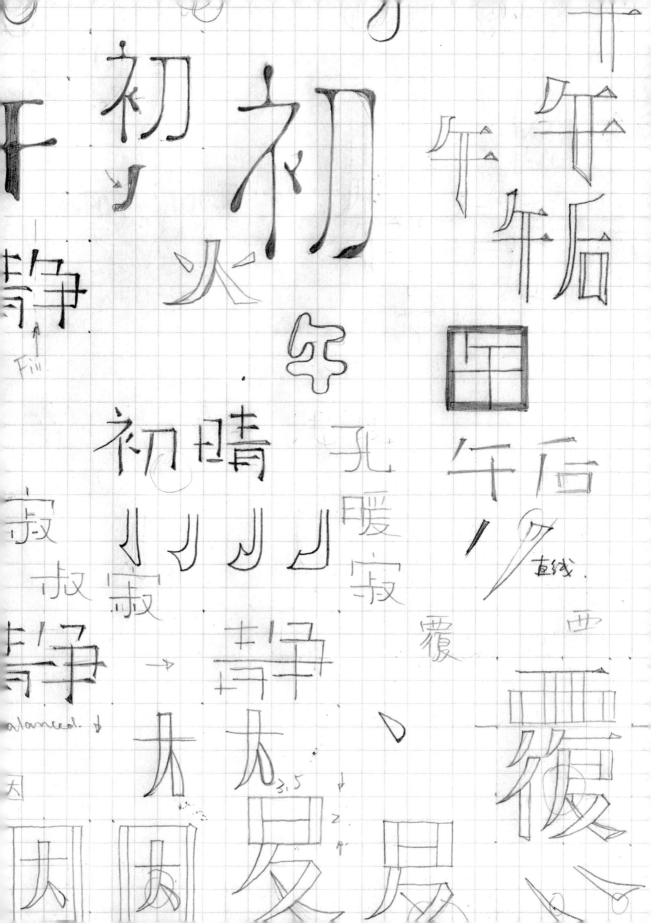

初 初 午
午
静 火 午后
午后

初晴 无 午后
寂 暖 午
寂 寂 直线
静 静 覆
因 大 大 圆 是

Лень и равнодушие

Alexandra Korolkova

Moscow • Russia

'Sketching is a very important stage for me when I need to design some lettering or display typeface close to calligraphy,' says typeface designer Alexandra Korolkova, winner of the 2013 Prix Charles Peignot. 'But when I design something for text, I tend not to draw by hand.'

Instead, she explains, she usually tries to find the right tone, or spirit, in the sketches. 'What I like most and find most helpful in sketching is that I can imagine the result at once,' she says, noting that it is much easier to draw or write some things by hand than to design them using Bézier curves without any prototype. She also likes the 'irregularities and live details that you can't predict, but can make use of during the working process'.

Alexandra studied drawing for 12 years, and prefers pens, pencils and markers on paper to the computer, but maintains that she's not a sketchbook person: 'I don't know why. I had three or four sketchbooks, but mostly I sketch on single sheets of paper – and then lose them once the work is done.'

Among her sketches is a Russian alphabet written with a broad-nib pen. 'Actually, humanist hands are not the most natural for Cyrillic script, as they don't have a historical prototype,' she notes. 'Cyrillic text and humanist writing can be difficult to put together.'

Alexandra decided to conduct an experiment, over the course of several months, during which everything that she wrote by hand, from notes to shopping lists, would be written in upright lowercase. The idea was to find 'as quick, easy and natural a way to write every letter as possible,' she says. 'After that I made some conclusions on writing the upright Cyrillic, and since then I use it for both theoretical and practical purposes.'

Куда идём мы с Пятачком-
Большой-большой секрет,
И не расскажем мы
о нём,
О нет, о нет, о нет!

Ку...
Бол...
И не
О не...

Арфа бесится вновь,
как штурвал цеппелина,
Оплавляется контур
в усталых руках,
Выдувает сирокко
за гривою львиной
Тонкий пепел песка
на горбатых боках,
Только я
не успеваю к тебе,
Я не успеваю
к тебе...

ананана

бнбнбнб

внвнвнв

гнгнгнг

днднднд

унунуну

орне

фнфнфнфн

хнхнхнх

цннцнцнц

енененен

ёнёнёнё

жнжнжнж

знзнзнз

нкнннни

чнчнчнч

шншнши

щнщнщн

ьнчнчнь

ыныныны

ьньньнь

33

йкйкйкйк
кнкнкнкнк
лнлнлнлнл
мнмнмнмнм
онононо

пнпнпн
рнрнрнр
снснснс
тнтнтн

энэнэнэ
юнюнюнюню
янянянянянян

А А
А Б Б

В
Г Г
Д Е
Ж

Irina Koryagina

New York • New York • USA

'It's hard to see how to succeed in hand-lettering without sketching, as opposed to typesetting,' says Siberian-born designer Irina Koryagina. 'I find it easier to pin down difficult curves quickly by hand, rather than by endless carpal tunnel-inducing pulling of Bézier curves on the computer screen.'

One reason for the appeal of sketching, Irina says, is that her sketchbook 'doesn't need a software update and won't crash at the least convenient moment'. She works with pens and Sharpies, exclusively in black and red, in sketchbooks, notepads and composition books – 'also, unfortunately, Post-its, none of which are deserving of being in a book'.

As a non-Latin script native user, Irina rediscovered the 'Yes' sketch (above) by going over her notes from a university course on Scientific Methodology. Of the drawing, she says, 'I hope there's at least one person out there who can read Russian and might be able to see more on this page than just the self-absorbed answers and amateur work of some unknown type aficionado.'

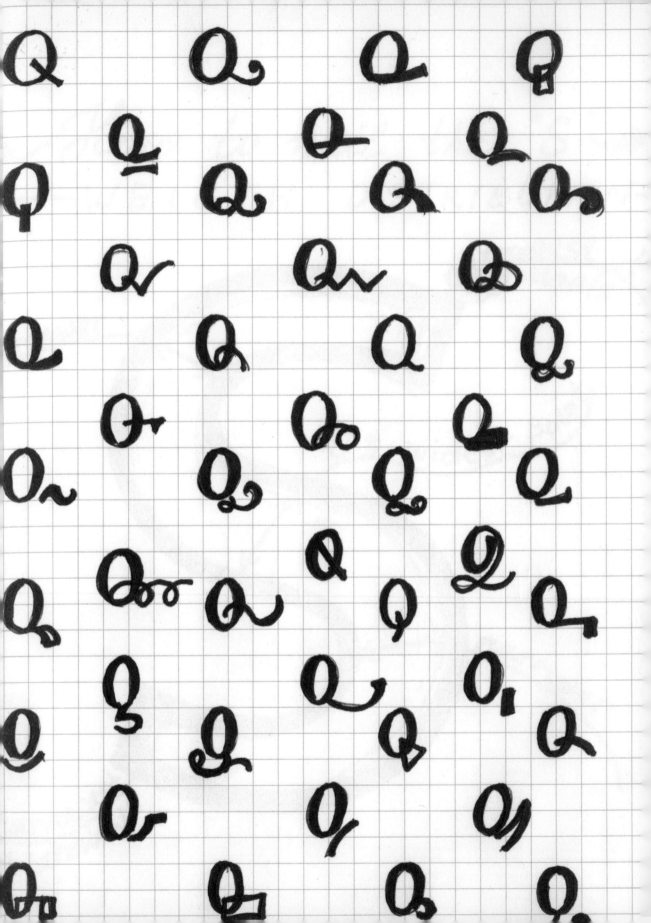

narrowest at
terminals

narrower

the widest point

Й Й Й Й

п

N N N N

Й Й

Henrik Kubel

London · UK

'Sketching has an unmatched energy –
it is raw and honest,' says Danish type
designer Henrik Kubel. 'Drawing by
hand allows me to make an immediate
recording of my thoughts. The core
concept develops from what remains
after everything has been refined
on the computer screen.'

Henrik admits that he will use
anything to draw, although he has
a preference for black Sharpie markers.
'I sketch on loose paper, envelopes,
Post-it notes, tablecloths, walls,
anything,' he says. 'Sometimes I collect
and glue all these thoughts, sketches,
ideas, marks, notes and mistakes into
sketchbooks. These can be years apart
– there is no system, as such. Sketching
directly into a book is too intimidating
for me. Each page has to be perfect.'

Henrik has even made a sketch on
a matchbox for a poster design
(opposite). The final poster was done
in one go with a spray can, and retains
the same energy as the original sketch.
'It is one of my favourite works,' he says.

Canadian based, illustrator, thinker, writer and typographer extraordinaire Marian Bantjes is giving a rare lecture at the Royal College of Art. Bantjes will discuss everything she has done to date. Don't miss! — Advance warning: *Marian may swear during her presentation!* / 1st April, 2010 — Time: 15:30. Place: *Performing Arts Lab, Stevens Building, 1st floor*

Sagmeister says: "Marian is one of the most innovative typographers [...] today. She understands how to evoke historical sense in the [...] and onwards into the future."

Sigrid Albert says: "You are doing just what the medieval monks did when they ill[...] letters with their immense attention to detail and passion, almost visibly grasp[...] a higher being / a higher state of being, however one wants to express it. I don't know [...] You're creating deeply spiritual typography which goes beyond religion."

Tom Lane

Liverpool · UK

'Sketching underpins my entire process,' says Tom Lane, aka Ginger Monkey. 'Without it, I just stare blankly into the abyss. Refining my designs by hand also keeps me open to introducing new things relatively quickly, and thinking the project through in more depth.'

Over the years, Tom has honed his sketches to reflect the final project as closely as possible. 'Sometimes they actually are the finished work,' he explains. 'It depends on what the client is after, or what I deem to be appropriate. Often the computer is a finishing tool. I try to limit the decision-making at the screen, as I find my work comes out better that way.'

When sketching, Tom is able to shut out everything else, which is liberating and satisfies a deep-rooted need to be good at drawing. 'I'm not sure exactly where that comes from,' he says. 'I didn't study art at school, and designed digitally for the first few years of my career, so drawing, and being good at it, is a fairly recent discovery.'

Tom scans his rough sketchbook drawings into the computer, lays down some guides in Adobe Illustrator, and then uses the printouts to create more polished artwork. 'I've experimented with inking up my designs after laying down pencil marks, but I'm now a straight-up pencil-and-paper man,' he explains. 'I've tried sketching on a tablet, but that didn't turn out very well.'

BASK

New York

BASK

New York

INNER SPACING
BIGGER 'NEW YORK'

SHADOW + LIGHT

NEW YORK

BASK

Est 1920

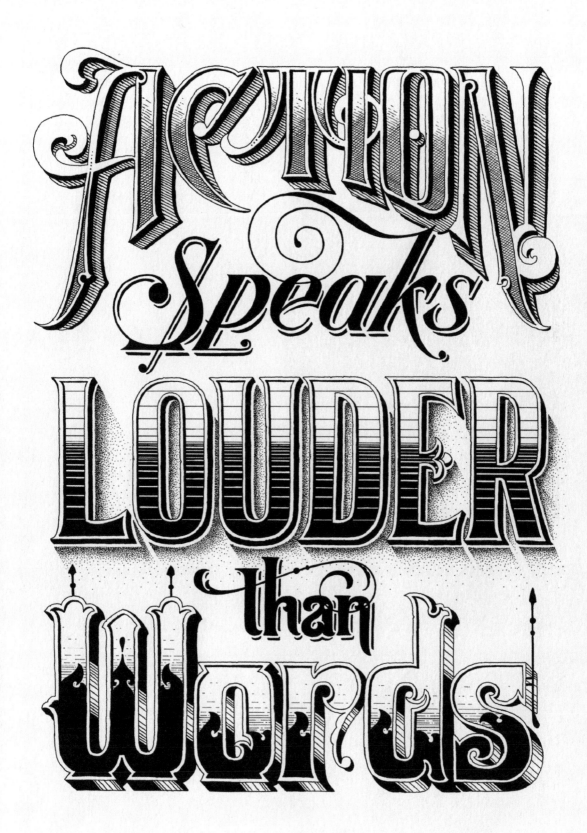

James Lunn

York • UK

'Sketching is fast and sometimes you can surprise yourself,' says designer James Lunn. When looking back over sketchbooks, he finds he will often come across previously discarded sketches that are relevant to a current project. 'It's a gratifying feeling to realize you weren't totally wrong, but just spitting out ideas for the future.'

Sketching allows James to quickly evaluate typographic ideas that are worth pursuing and those that aren't. 'I generally move to a computer quite quickly if I like something and build more detailed sketches from there,' he explains. 'But if it is proving difficult to visualize, I will work it out in my sketchbook just to make sure I understand exactly what it is I want to produce.'

While sketching can speed things up, nothing James draws in his sketchbook will ever be seen as the final piece. Using a sketchbook, he says, is like using any other tool, as 'it allows me to communicate with myself at the beginning of a project'. His tools are a combination of whatever medium best suits the intended outcome.

'If I am just doodling, I will mainly use a biro, as that is usually what is lying around. I struggle with using a sketchbook in a chronological way, as sometimes, because of its form, I can be a little precious about what goes in there. I tend to grab a pile of A4 sheets from the printer and not worry about what things look like. If it's wrong, I move on to the next sheet. At the end of a project, I will often just throw these in the bin.'

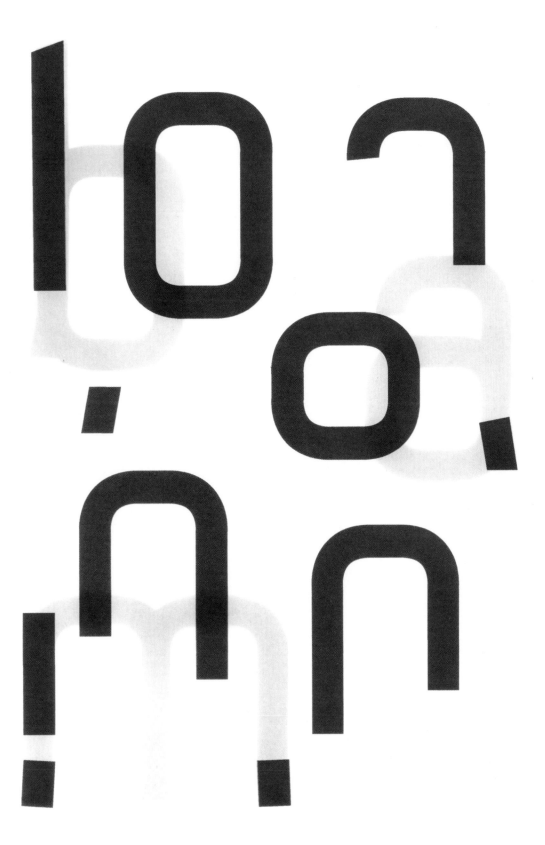

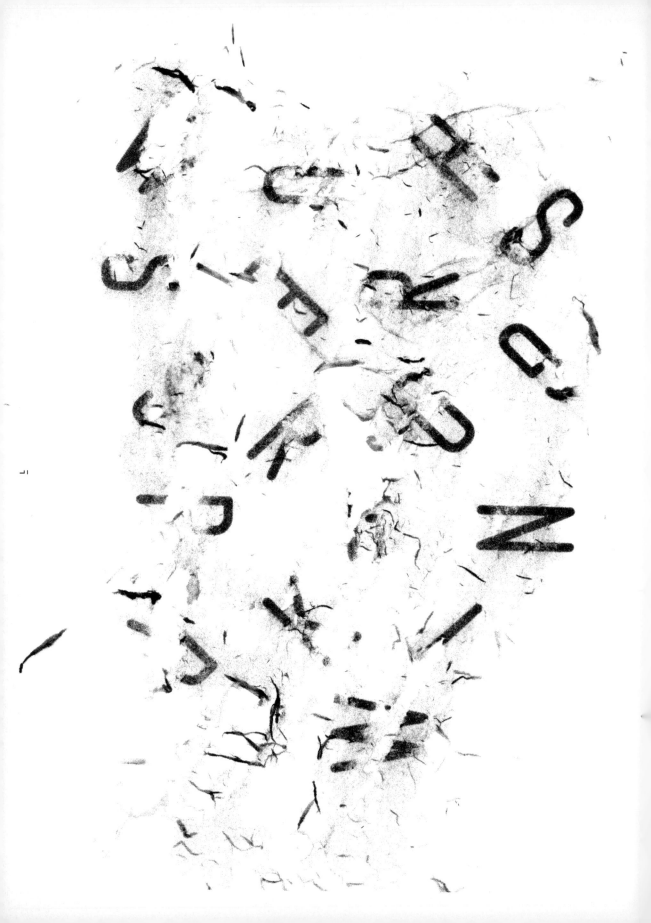

Pete McCracken

Portland · Oregon · USA

When asked if sketching is part of his normal routine, Pete McCracken replies: 'Yes and no: I tend to sketch to solve creatively the task at hand.' He may only work on something for a few minutes or an hour, but, he says, 'I don't sit down and sketch on a regular basis. It's a very irregular process, because I get bored doing one thing for too long.'

There are many different reasons why Pete, who runs a few foundries, uses sketching to keep his hand-eye skills in good form, from working through ideas quickly to solving a logistical issue. 'Before I began using a computer, I did everything by hand, because that was

the only way to do things,' he explains. 'I was definitely on the cusp of the desktop revolution, the transition from paste-up, phototypesetting, Letraset and stat camera PMTs.'

At times, his sketches become illegible. Looking over old sketchbooks, even Pete is not always able to decipher what he was trying to achieve. 'I also sketch to generate ideas, and have found that I will usually create something completely without intention, steering me down an entirely different path. This type of divergent brainstorming is what I look for when I sketch – not necessarily just on paper, but also when I am working through many different type, logo or layout ideas on the computer.'

To a large degree, sketching only affects finished work when Pete is trying to create a more natural-looking organic or weathered feel, something that's

hard to fake digitally: a line quality that softens with textural wobbliness, which you can't get from a computer. 'I'll create something as a sketch and keep working it and working it until I feel it's ready to be digitized,' he says.

What he likes most about sketching is that it is very mutable. Every gesture, either making a mark or erasing, will be different. 'Sketching is as much about removing as it is about making a mark,' he says. 'Even though sketching can be about moulding or sculpting, there is a degree of finality that doesn't happen on the computer, because you can't just make an exact copy. Each time you sketch something freehand that's supposed to be the same, it will be slightly different in some aspect. At least, that's what happens to me.'

Doug Fir

Brookland
OREGON

Brookland
OREGON

Doug Fir

Portlyn
NEW YORK

Elegant design

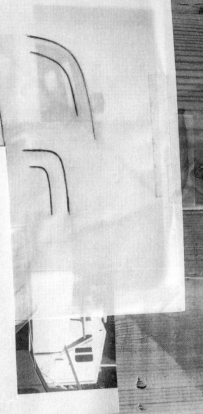

HOD
dood
REI

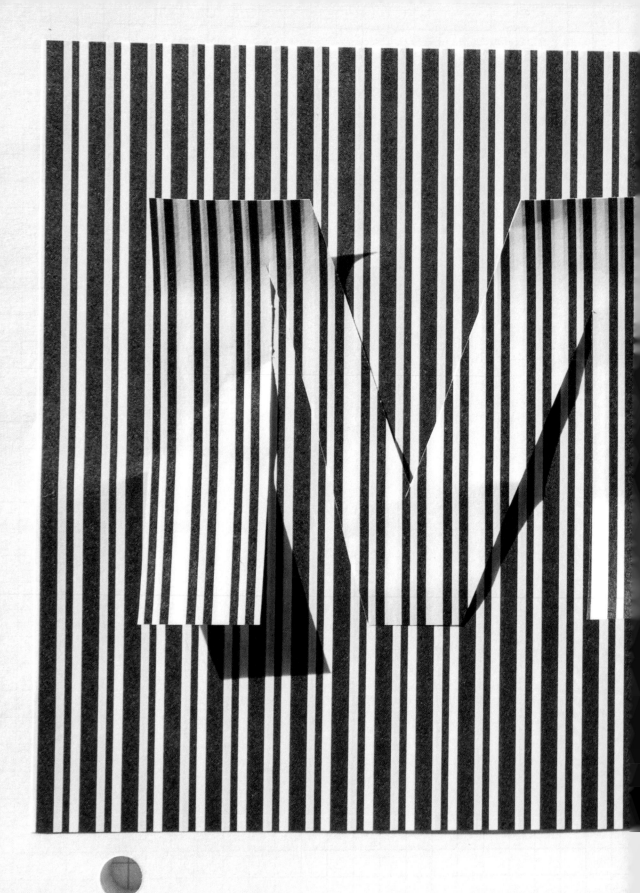

Pablo A. Medina

Brooklyn • New York • USA

Sketching is a form of meditation for designer Pablo A. Medina, who founded the graphic design studio Design is Culture in Brooklyn in 2014. 'It is a way of eliciting deep concentration, relaxation and healing,' he says. 'I use all of the tools at my disposal. The thing that I'm making determines the medium and tool I use – in sketchbooks mostly, but I've been known to deface a bathroom wall or two.'

For Pablo, his sketches 'have their own process. They start loose and gestural, and then become more refined. The last sketch before the final execution is a type of dress rehearsal,' he says, 'where I get to practise and feel free to make mistakes.'

Pablo's sketches for the Pen Is Mightier Than The Machine Gun project were drawn in response to the *Charlie Hebdo* shootings in Paris in 2015 – just one of hundreds of journal entries he has created. 'They contain my deepest, darkest thoughts,' he says.

E

CONFLI
AND
CONFU
SION

THERE IS SO M
LOV
IN TH
CIT

Finally, I HAVE A

UCH

THE OCE AN IS SI NGING for a fe w Day

Laura
Meseguer

Barcelona • Spain

Freelance type designer Laura
Meseguer, who specializes in branding
and editorial projects, is inspired,
she says, 'by the inherent beauty and
integrity of letterforms, and their ability
to express emotions'.

For Laura, drawing and sketching
are one and the same. 'I use drawing
as a tool for expression,' she explains,
but the results will take on different
forms. 'When I work on lettering, the
end result is pretty close to the final
drawing, I begin with calligraphy, and
then draw on top with tracing paper.
Later, I will make some adjustments
when digitizing.'

Her first extensive typeface family,
'Multi', was originally commissioned in
2011, and she has recently expanded it
with 'MultiText' and 'MultiDisplay'. 'Qandus
Latin', the typeface she developed as
part of Typographic Matchmaking In The
Maghrib, the third incarnation of the
Khatt Foundation's multi-script research
project, will be released as an extended
version in 2018.

Espress

noivacrt

noivacrt

Mrs. Lilien

The Art

TWO COLOR
CROMATIC   TYPEFACE

A B C D E F
G H I J K L
M N O P Q R S T U V W X Y Z

STREET

HAFINS KINSTER
HAUS MEISTER·SO RE·
ELIXIER EVERW AND
ANDTSCEN QUE PEL X
DAS HIER FOLGENDI
LICHEN STAUNEN
DAS BERG+DAS BER
NICHTS WARAND+
LEUCHTS WARAND

GOD
ONLY
knows

GOD
ONLY
knows

Niels Shoe Meulman

Amsterdam · Netherlands

'The joy of sketching,' says former graffiti artist and muralist Niels Shoe Meulman, 'lies in the freedom and possibilities it offers and the ability to surprise yourself when your hand produces strokes you couldn't foresee in your imagination. Sketches are a way of checking your head: is an idea going to work in reality?'

Shoe identifies three types of sketching: paper to paper, paper to digital, and paper to canvas. 'Back in the days when a typographic design would be deliverable as a stat print, I would trace a sketch dozens of times until it was perfect,' he explains. 'But when the Mac came along, there was a point at which you would decide to digitalize and finalize. Still, I love Bézier curves a lot less than before. These days I only sketch

for murals and paintings. The sketches are much rougher. If the message is clear, and I know the composition of letters and strokes, it's time to attack the surface. Let accidents happen. I guess I became experienced enough to not need a detailed plan.'

Shoe notes that he always tries to sketch in notebooks, because pieces of paper have a tendency to disappear. He's currently on book no. 59 (he began numbering his sketchbooks in, he thinks, about 1994). 'They contain a mixture of sketches and written ideas,' he says. 'But for me, painting and writing are the same thing.'

The wall Shoe created for ST+ART India in Delhi (p. 202) is a good example of the 'symbiosis' he feels he is 'beginning to own – writing the poetry and composing the words at the same time, keeping the wall's holes and ridges in mind. I write paintings and I paint words, but that's nothing new – I've been doing that since my graffiti days, back in the 1980s!'

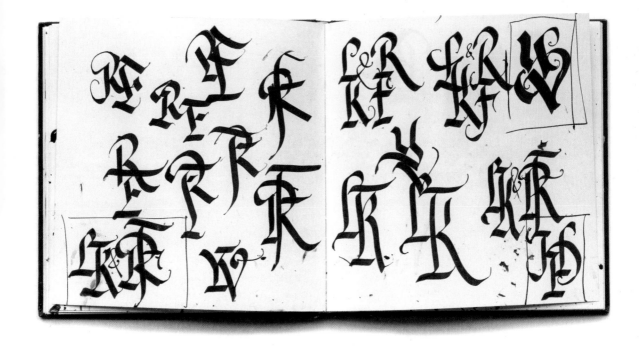

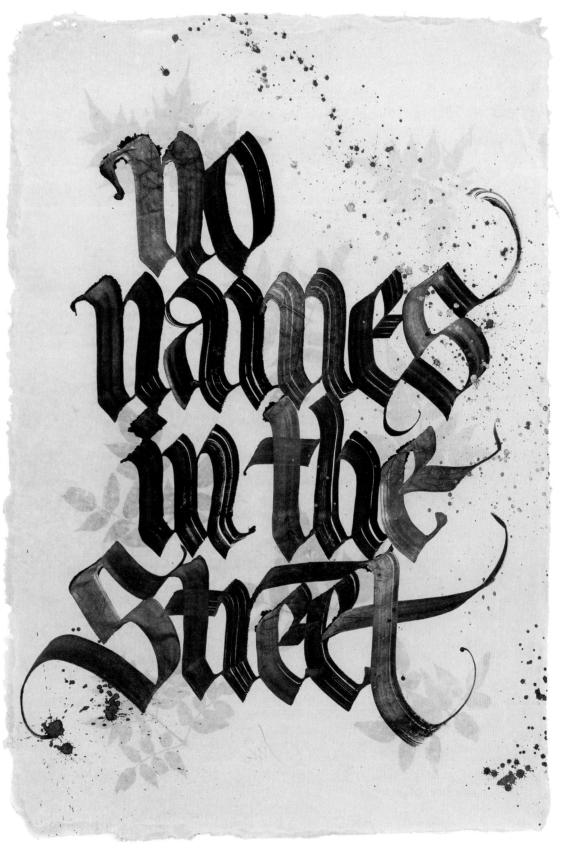

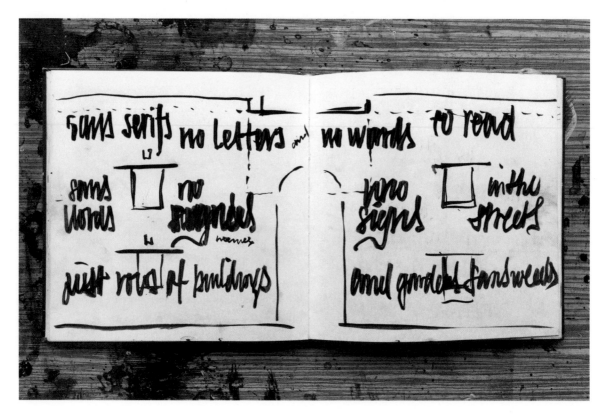

Thomas Milo

Amsterdam · Netherlands

The work of Thomas Milo, who set up DecoType with Mirjam Somers, a fellow specialist in Arabic type, is always derived directly from original manuscript models. This is seen particularly in the classic typefaces Ruq'ah, Naskh, Persian and Pakistani Nasta'liq.

'We analyse and create minimal subletter shapes digitally,' Thomas explains. 'Recently, a type historian concluded that we simply digitized the existing metal typefaces of Ohannis Mühendis-oglu, an Ottoman Armenian printer who created a metal typeface based on the same kind of Naskh manuscript style in the 1860s. None of the original sorts remain, to my knowledge. It's a great example of how one can round off an observation to the nearest perceptional mismatch, based on legacy technology.'

What makes this amusing, he says, 'is that DecoType's raison d'être is a radical departure from conventional pre-digital typographic concepts. So instead of digitizing existing solutions – as the mainstream industry did when basing itself on metal and phototypesetting practice – we went straight for the manuscript sources. Nor did we aspire to create novel impressions of Arabic shapes: we approach typography not as a personal artistic expression, but as a way of modelling writing traditions in order to make them available for academic and literary book production.'

330

141

06BE

42

150

—150
—564 → niet kof
— alles

L   M   K

| 1111 |
| 1163 |
| 1012 |

en   L   M   J   K

23 sp
98

641

98 sp
23 sp
98
98 sp

| 1005 |
| 1000 |
| 1121 |
| 1092 |

11
12
11
12
11 | 201 alles, geen gesl. meem

289 06CI
291 F6CI

M   0645   F645

— b-m jeem, b-feh, b-seen, b-beh, m-beh
b-lam, 06BE, b-sad, b-heh, b-m-ain
b-m-kaf, b-meem   —570 [— b-meem

— mfeh, msad, b-ulah 3× m-meem
b-heh, y-heh ZW2 kesh 06BE F68E ZW2 —570 [— b-lam 201
06BE

— m-lam, naar alles, m-2sp seen,

[— m-lam → niet daal bl.

100 — — sp   —724 [
-120

sp [— sp   —549 [25, 452
kesh ZW2   F68E 256
—570 [452 804, 415, 25, 271 127

— b-m-jeem, b-feh, m-lam, b-m-kaf, b-ain
m-ain, b-heh, 06BE → K (ZW2)

— idem maar: m-lam K

— b-lam, b-beh, b-seen, b-sad, b-meem [m-lam → daal bl. kkns
201 | 23, 23, 23 (60) 259 [en alle andere
202 K
m-seen

— m-sad, b-m-tah, b, b,
06 F68E, b-heh, kesh, y-heh, m-feh,
m-beh, ZW2.   sp [sp

b k 259 uren   e 60 uren   (60 isook sl. vo- y naar b-meem)
let op sl. 192 en 520 misschien is verschil niet meer ...

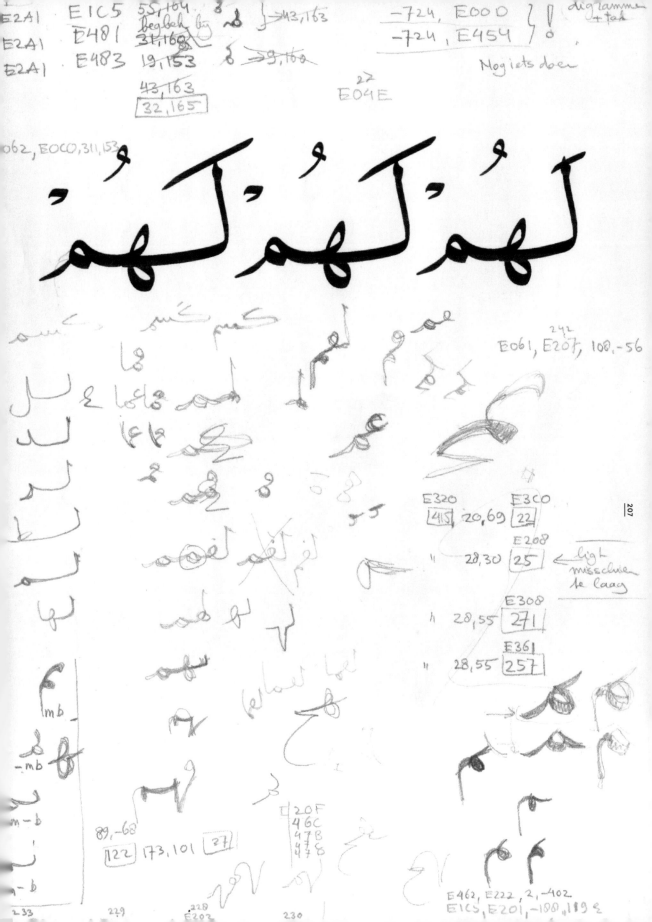

Flavio Morais

Barcelona • Spain

Sketching 'gives the soul to the finished work', says Brazilian illustrator Flavio Morais, now based in Spain. 'The process of sketching allows me to discover ideas that would otherwise be unlikely.' Like so many other designers, what Flavio likes best about sketching is the spontaneity.

This spontaneity comes through in his choice of tool – a marker pen on couche (coated) paper, sketchbook pages or 'any dirty surface'. Flavio is philosophical about sketching. Quoting the painter John Singer Sargent, he says, 'you can't do sketches enough: sketch everything, and keep your curiosity fresh.'

ELECTRO

NEGÃO
e seus
AFRICAN

CHORIZO

TAPAS
SELECTAS
Café

São João
S. JOÃO Nº 6
VIVA!

rojão
24 de junho
curau

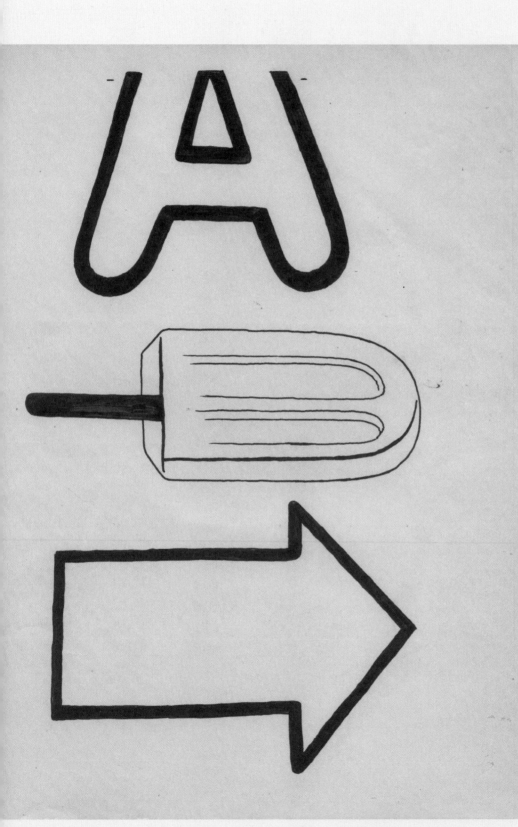

PÍAUÍ

EL SOCORRO - SAN GIL - CHARALÁ - MAGOTES -

COLOMBIA 14

LANCHES

NO REINO DO VAI NÃO VEM

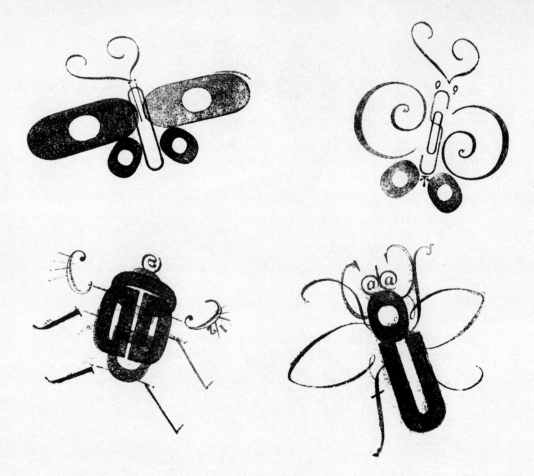

Bill Moran

Two Rivers · Wisconsin · USA

For Bill Moran of the Hamilton Wood Type and Printing Museum in Wisconsin, sketching is a way to document his thought process. 'At the same time,' he says, 'I try not to be a slave to the sketch. There's an important evolution that takes place between it and the finished print. You have to leave room in the creative process for change.'

Bill's sketches tend to focus on typeface selection and scale. 'I work strictly with wood and metal type, and am limited to what I have on hand,' he explains. 'I like that limitation, because it forces me to be more creative. When I don't have the right size available, I improvise by drawing the letterform on a piece of plywood, cutting out the shape on a bandsaw and stuffing it full of lead type to create a new letterform.' His favourite part of the process is 'getting it over with and inking up the press. That's where the fun happens.'

Bill uses fine-tip felt markers for his drawings, but also 'sketches' with a small proofing press that has been in his family since the 1930s. 'I can place the type at wonky angles, overprint multiple times and repeat letterforms to build up textures. Of course, you can do a lot of that on the computer, but the computer can't reveal the beauty of wet ink or the tonnage of a Chandler & Price printing press.'

'Letterbugs' (shown here) began as a concept for an art-crawl poster in 2001. The idea turned out to be a bottomless well of possibilities, fed by presses and type that Bill had hanging around for decades. When he began to work for the museum, the possibilities expanded exponentially. 'I feel really lucky that I found a motif I can continue to explore as an artist and printmaker,' he says.

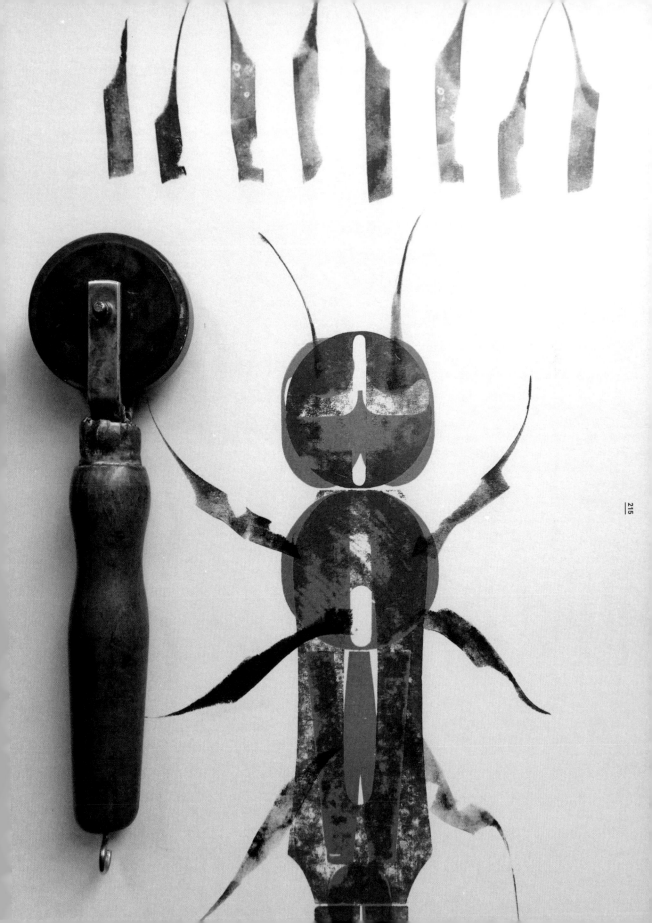

Dmitri Moruz

Moscow • Russia

For type designer Dmitri Moruz, sketching is a starting point, from which the designs are taken further in the digital environment until they are eventually finalized. 'Sketching is thinking made visual,' he says. 'I honestly don't know how it impacts my work, but I hope my designs are improved because of it.'

Sketching is a quick and accessible tool for generating ideas and concepts. An added benefit, Dmitri notes, is that 'a sketchbook doesn't have a battery, so it never dies'. Sketching also suits his favourite 0.7 mm Caran d'Ache red metal pencil. His sketchbook is equally low tech: 'I have a Muji notebook with clean, somewhat yellowish pages. But for a quick ideas sketch, anything works. I don't sketch on napkins, however: it is a "mission impossible" if you try.'

Most of the sketches shown here illustrate the development process of Dmitri's 'Molda Bold' typeface, created as a self-initiated project during the four-week Type As Language course at the School of Visual Arts in New York. It is based on the letterforms of an old form of Moldavian currency, from the early 1990s.

'When it was time to draw currency symbols,' Dmitri explains, 'I realized that Moldavian currency didn't have a symbol of its own. Suddenly the project turned into creating a currency symbol for the keys. It was fun.'

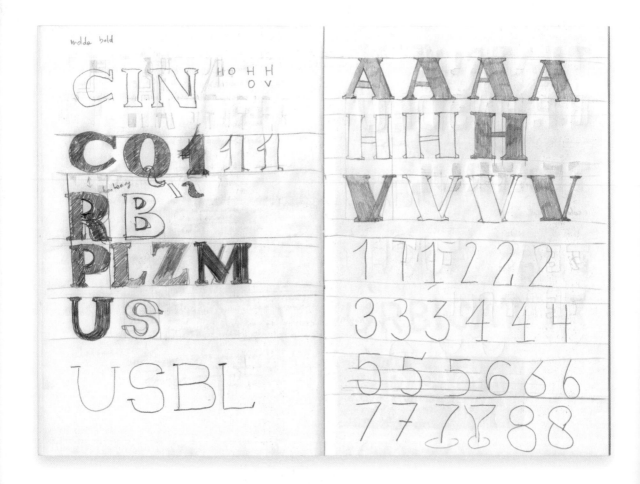

MOLDA BOLD TYPEFACE SERIES
DMITRI MORUZ, 2015

MOLDA BOLD TYPEFACE SERIES
DMITRI MORUZ, 2015

7L

8L

We've
been
waiting
for you

WELCOME
TO MOLDOVA

WELCOME
TO MOLDOVA

VISIT
MOLDOVA

TEATRUL B.P. HASDEU

2 shade tope stencil

TEATRUL

1 color stencil

mushroom

urbica design

urbica

URBICA

URBICA
A
URBICA

URBICA
↑ слишком просто

URBICA
RIR

URBICA ÆR

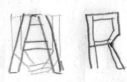

Joachim Müller-Lancé

San Francisco · California · USA

'I try to corral ideas in without defining them too early,' says Swiss designer Joachim Müller-Lancé, 'checking their viability while hopefully leaving enough rope. Before art school, I believed, naively, that the artist envisions the whole design in his mind, and then draws it onto paper. But the only time I succeeded in doing that the result was boring. It is experimentation that leads to unexpected new findings.'

For fixing an idea quickly any tool is fine, but for working out a more intricate concept, Joachim prefers a pen that can respond to pressure, so that he can begin light and loose, then go progressively darker to highlight or flesh out details, or draw over a mistake. A fine tip is good for adding details, annotations, and so on, later.

'Sketching is the first reality check for the images in my head, so getting an idea down on paper reveals whether it is worth pursuing,' he says. 'Admittedly, sketching also allows me to continue embellishing a mediocre concept until it looks worthy, which is why I try to keep it quick and utilitarian. If I have nothing at hand to draw with, I write my thoughts down, but follow that up with drawing as soon as I can.'

Joachim wants the final piece to retain some traces of his 'search for form', so the viewer understands the process. 'When the end product is digital,' he says, 'I move on to the computer as quickly as possible, and continue sketching and experimenting onscreen. If I make very tight paper sketches, then scan and trace them as vectors, the resulting shapes can look surprisingly overwrought. I have no idea if this happens to other type designers, but have seen it in some illustrators' and cartoonists' work.'

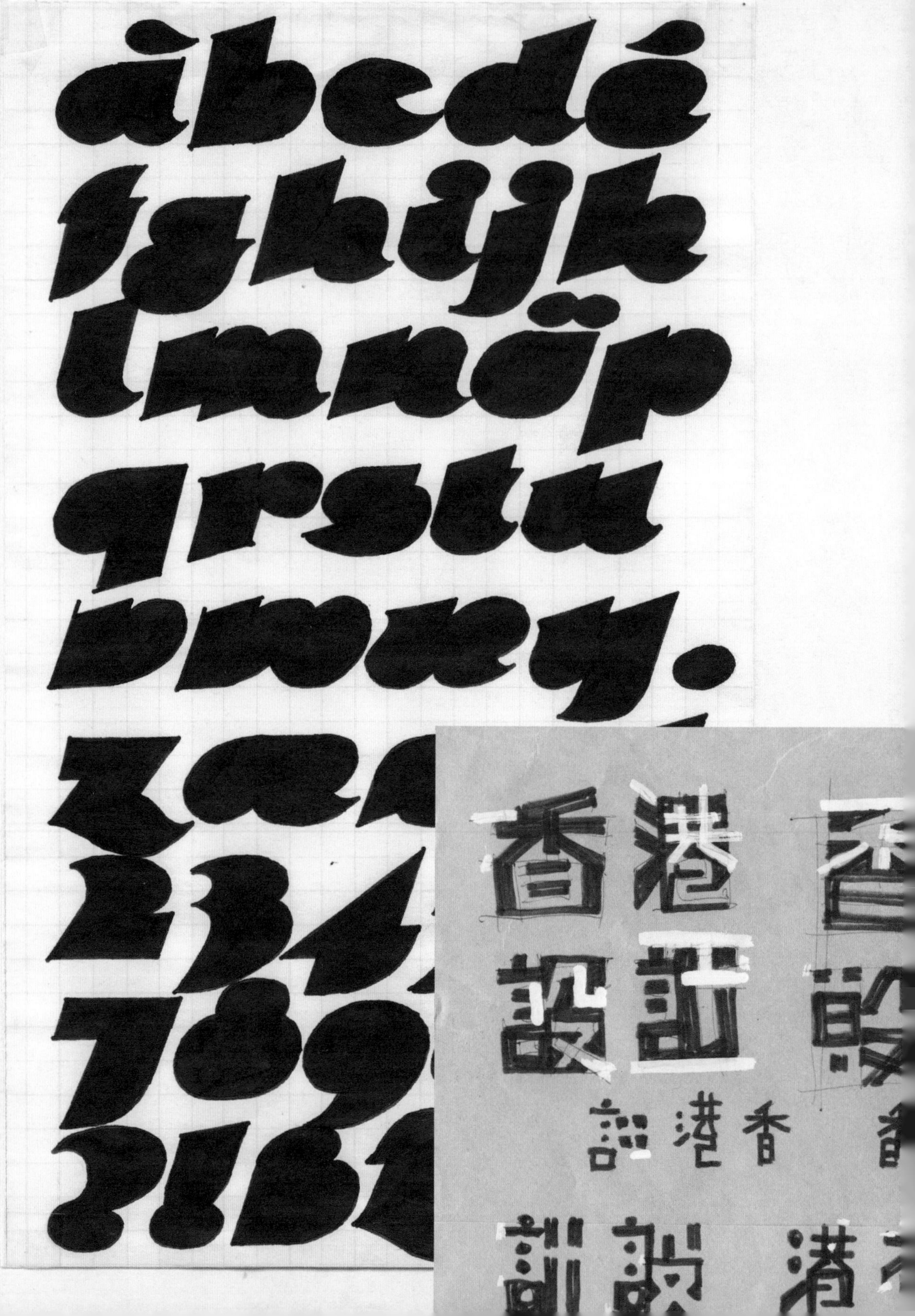
香港
設計

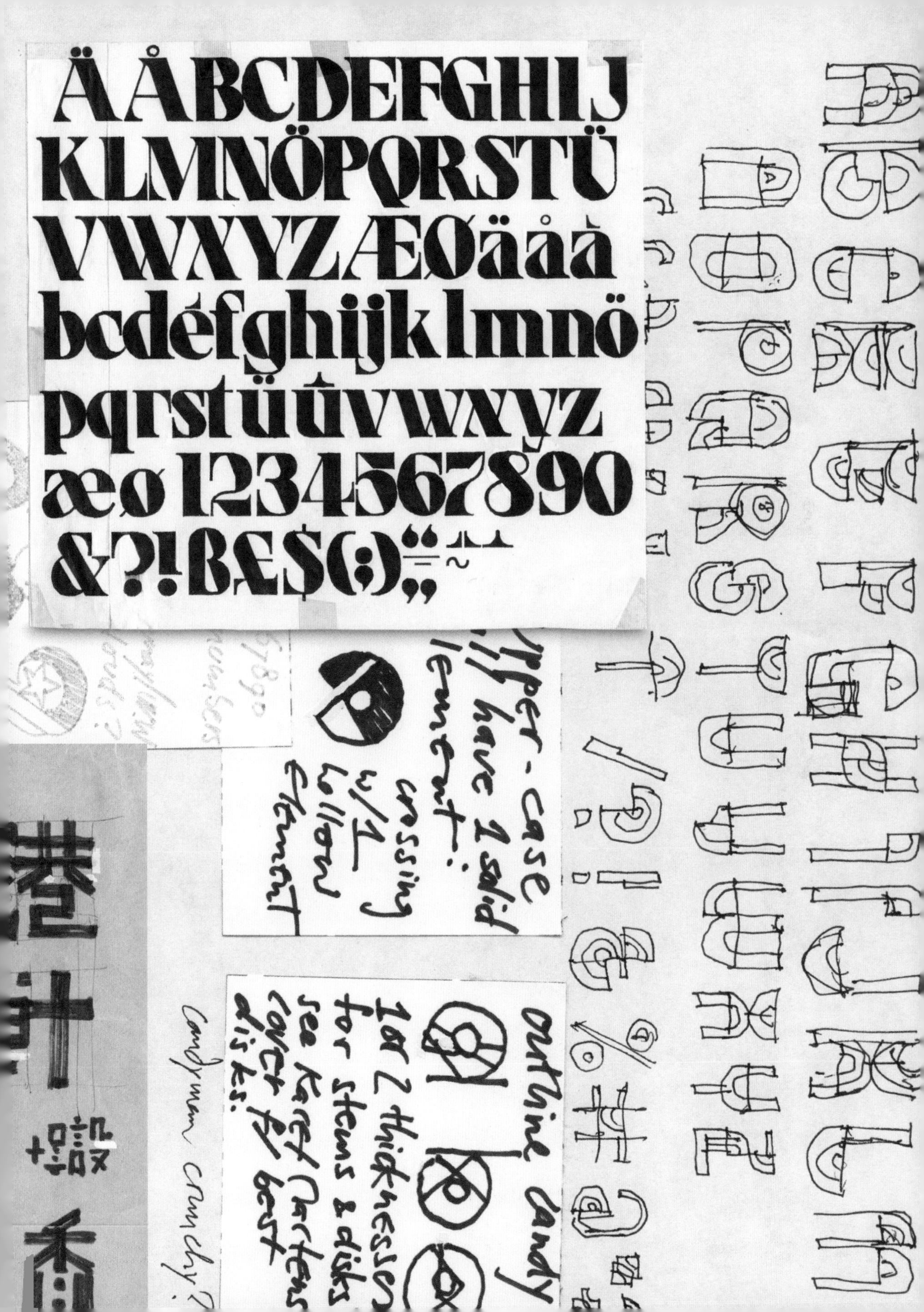

ÄÅABCDEFGHIJ
KLMNÖPQRSTÜ
VWXYZÆŒØäåã
bcdéfghijklmnö
pqrstüûvwxyz
æø1234567890
&?!ßBEŞ(.)„„ ̃

Morag Myerscough

London · UK

Muralist Morag Myerscough tends
to do her sketching at the beginning
of a project, when, she says, she wants
to get some initial thoughts on paper.
'Being away from the computer with
just a pen, some coloured stickers
and a plain sheet of paper, sometimes
with a square grid, helps to loosen
up my thoughts,' she adds.

Making those first marks is not easy,
however. 'It takes a lot out of me to
begin sketching,' Morag continues.
'I have to choose the right moment,
and then the sketches usually form the
basis for large installation pieces.' She
uses pens, pencils, stickers and felt-tip
markers in an array of colours. 'I buy lots
of various shapes of stickers, as well as
those I print myself, and have a large pile
of items around me to work with.'

Morag's preferred drawing surface is
Bristol paper or square-grid notebooks.
'When I am in meetings I like to sketch
type, and it gives me a great base to
work with,' she explains. 'And when
I work on sketches for my installations
I will use an A3 pad of Bristol paper.'

For the Temple of Agape project
(right), Morag incorporated 69 words
from Martin Luther King, Jr's 1967
speech 'Where Do We Go From Here'.
She recalls: 'I was on a two-hour train
journey out of London, and since I
had brought my sketch materials with
me, I just started drawing. I kept going
and going. When I finished, I thought,
this is it! The next day I sent it to the
Southbank Centre, and they just said,
"Yes!" So we made it.'

225

LOOK
AGAIN!

▽▽

WHAT
ARE
YOU
LOOKINK
AT.

AGAIN

LOOK
△▽
SEE

130 x £100

WHAT DO YOU SEE

ILLUM INKAFE EYE.

MOVE THE ROUND.

LOOK

DRAWING EASELD.

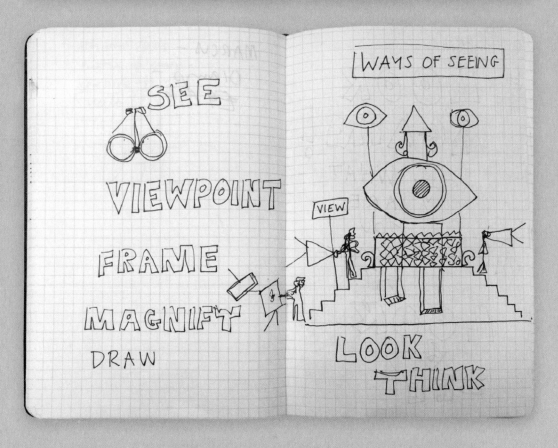

SEE

VIEWPOINT

FRAME

MAGNIFY

DRAW

WAYS OF SEEING

VIEW

LOOK
THINK

S Z

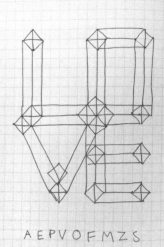

AEPVOFMZS

2ND JAN 2015

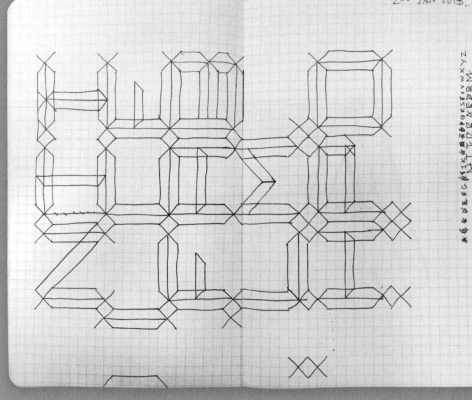

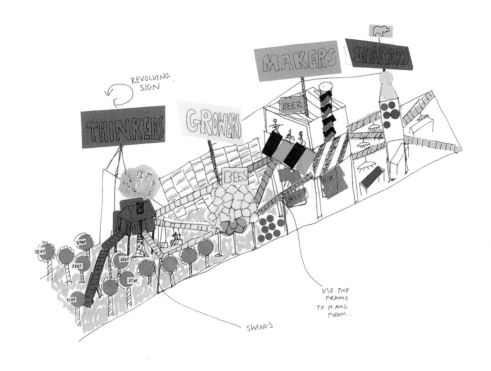

a bcdefghijklmnopqrstuvwxyyz
a q g d b p p 1234567890

ABCDEFGHIJKLMNOPQRSTUVWXYZ

ABCDEFGHIJKLPLMNOPQR

STTUVWXYZ

A N Sander Blad Vormgeving
Vakantie Semnadisse Rimondeix
Ge Gueret Gouzon

Sander Neijnens

Tilburg • Netherlands

Sander Neijnens's 'TilburgsAns' typeface was inspired, he says, by the character of the Dutch city of Tilburg. It is a large metropolitan centre, with a theatre, university and museum of modern art, but it also has the compactness of a small village.

As a result, Sander says, 'I decided to design a typeface that has the characteristics of both printed type and handwriting, and began by sketching letters with a fine marker, then scanning the results and turning them into outlines. The outlines were then straightened to make the design more rational and efficient. At a certain point I stopped refining, as otherwise the design would lose its personality. The result is a typeface that is still connected to handwriting, but can be used for more than just a short line of text.'

Sander always begins with an overall idea, before refining it. Sketching, he says, is an important tool for trying out various options. Pen and pencil are in the main his choice at the beginning of a project, because he can work quickly and express his ideas 'in a natural way'.

Later on, the computer becomes a convenient means of comparing several variations of a design. 'The first sketches remain a point of reference for the final work,' he explains. 'In other words, if the final work isn't at least as good as the sketch, you're not ready.'

He continues: 'Sketching gives form to an idea. A vague notion is transformed into a concrete drawing, which creates the opportunity to judge it.' Sander once bought a sketchbook to take with him on travels and holidays, but only used three pages: 'I prefer any piece of paper that's available the moment I get an idea.'

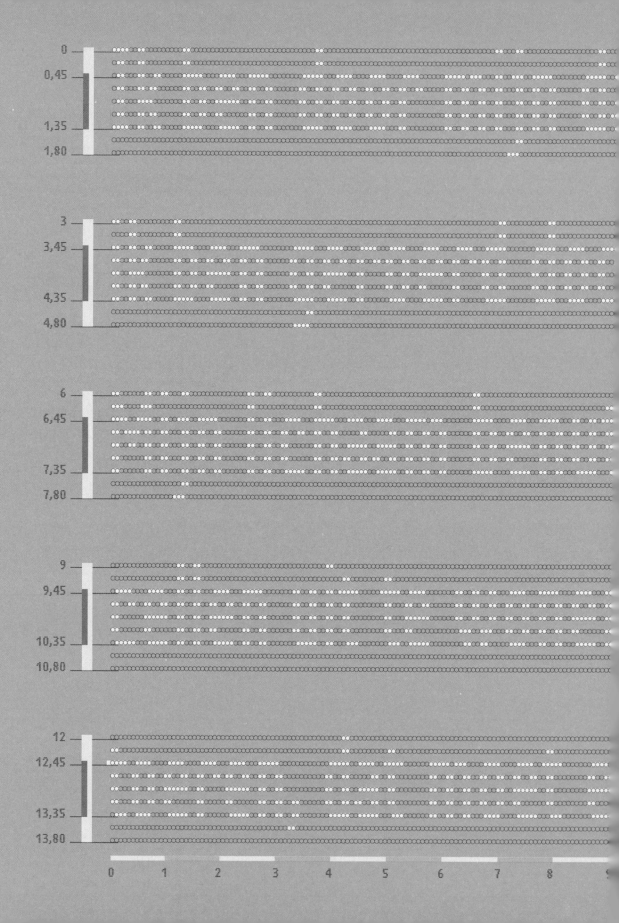

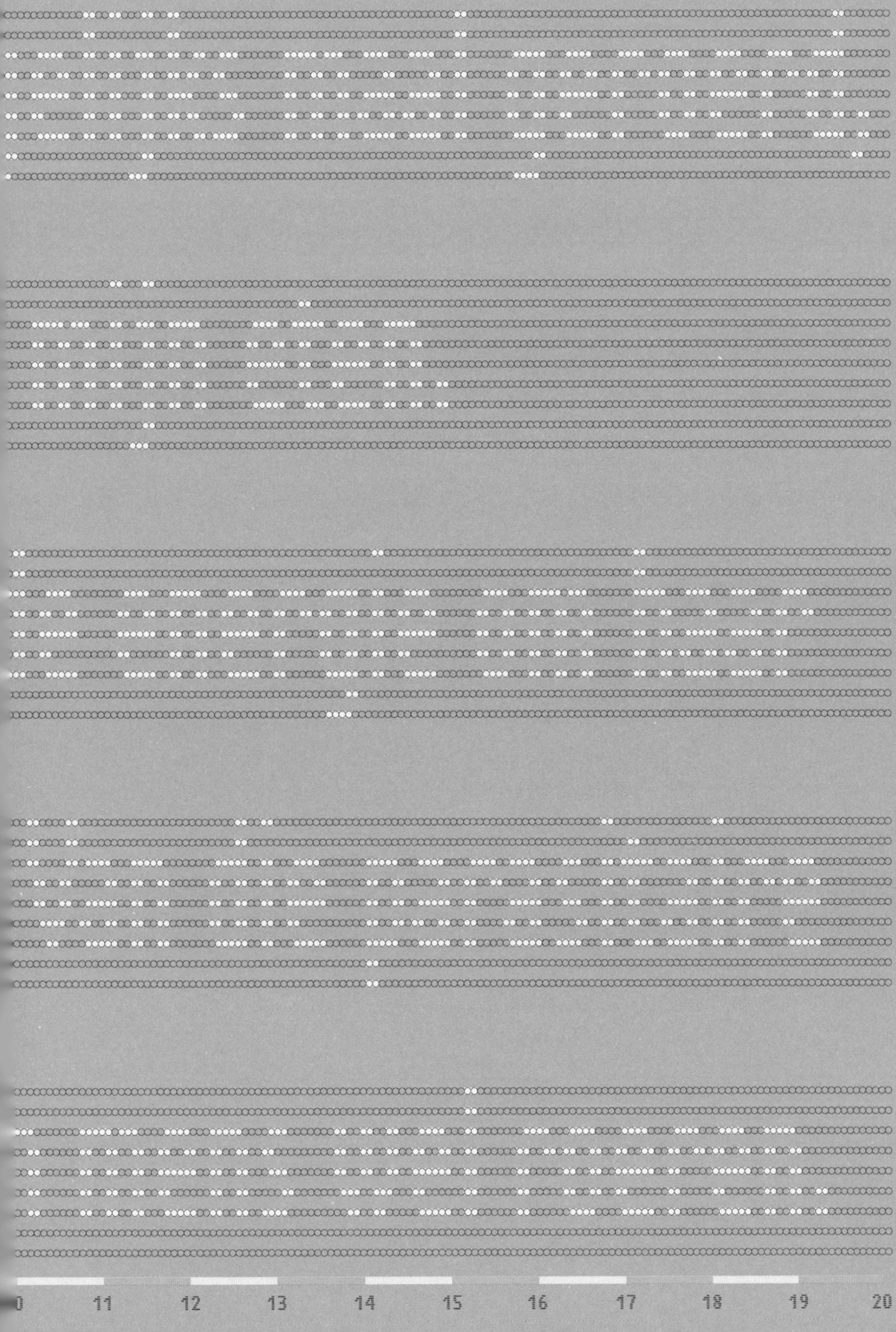
0
11
12
13
14
15
16
17
18
19
20

Jovan Shpira Obradovic

Novi Sad • Serbia

It is the physical aspect of sketching – making quick drawings just to see how things will look – which appeals to Jovan Shpira Obradovic. 'When it comes to my design job, sketching is always essential, since a lot of the stuff I do is quite digital: web design, print, and so on,' he explains.

Jovan's preference is for pencils, working in sketchbooks or on sheets of A4 paper. 'When I do work that has to do with typography, I usually make sketches,' he explains. 'The things I usually do for myself – street art and graffiti – are mostly hand-drawn, so I make sketches for those projects.'

The Skeleton Typography Project illustrated here was developed for Knowyourself.com. There was no demand to make typographic illustrations by hand when Jovan joined the team, but, he says, 'I figured it would be really cool if the typography was done by hand first, and then drawn in vectors. That way it would have another feeling, other than just digital. They had some photos of a plaster skeleton, as a reference, so I printed those on a printer, and then drew the sketches over it.'

As the project developed, Jovan says, 'the client loved how it turned out, and wanted some of the sketches sent to them, so that they could have them framed and hung on the wall. I also made an exhibition of the project in my hometown, and some of the sketches were a part of that, too.'

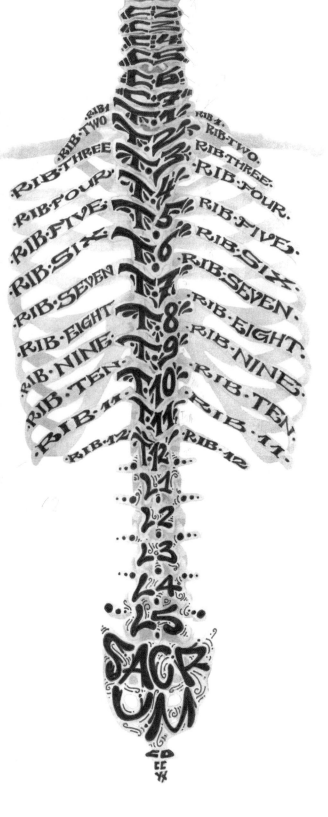

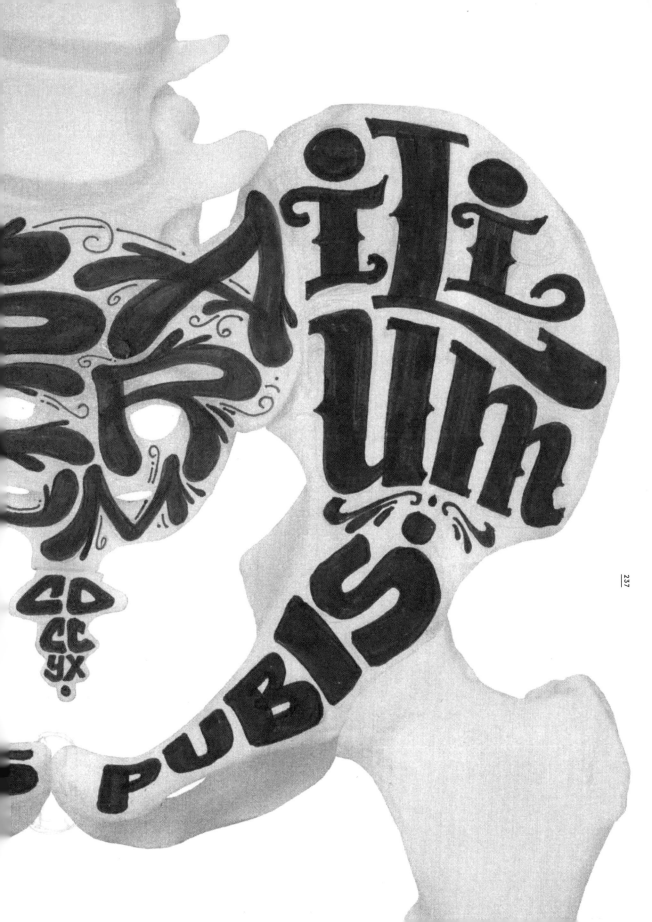

ILIUM

SACRUM

COCCYX

PUBIS

ISCHIUM

01

Jayme Odgers

Los Angeles • California • USA

In making his text-based paintings, postmodernist guru Jayme Odgers does not make sketches for working out details. 'I use sketches to record my thoughts,' he says. 'If I don't record them in some fashion, they vanish – often forever.'

Sketching does vary the overall impact of his finished work, however. 'Occasionally an idea sketch might closely represent the final painting, but for the most part they only record an initial thought,' Jayme explains. He prefers to work out details and corrections in the final work, leaving, he says, 'considerable *pentimenti*'. These, he says, 'give a sense of life to the finished product, which can otherwise appear rather static'.

Jayme enjoys the immediacy of sketching, noting that a drawing often has more life than the end result. 'Of course, some ideas or concepts require one tool over another to realize them properly,' he says, 'but if I had to pick one tool above all others, it would be the pencil for its flexibility and immediacy. I *love* pencils.'

Jayme does not use sketchbooks, preferring instead to draw on individual sheets of paper, so that he can rearrange the order if necessary. 'I prefer archival paper,' he says, 'because the sketch often becomes a final work.'

GER

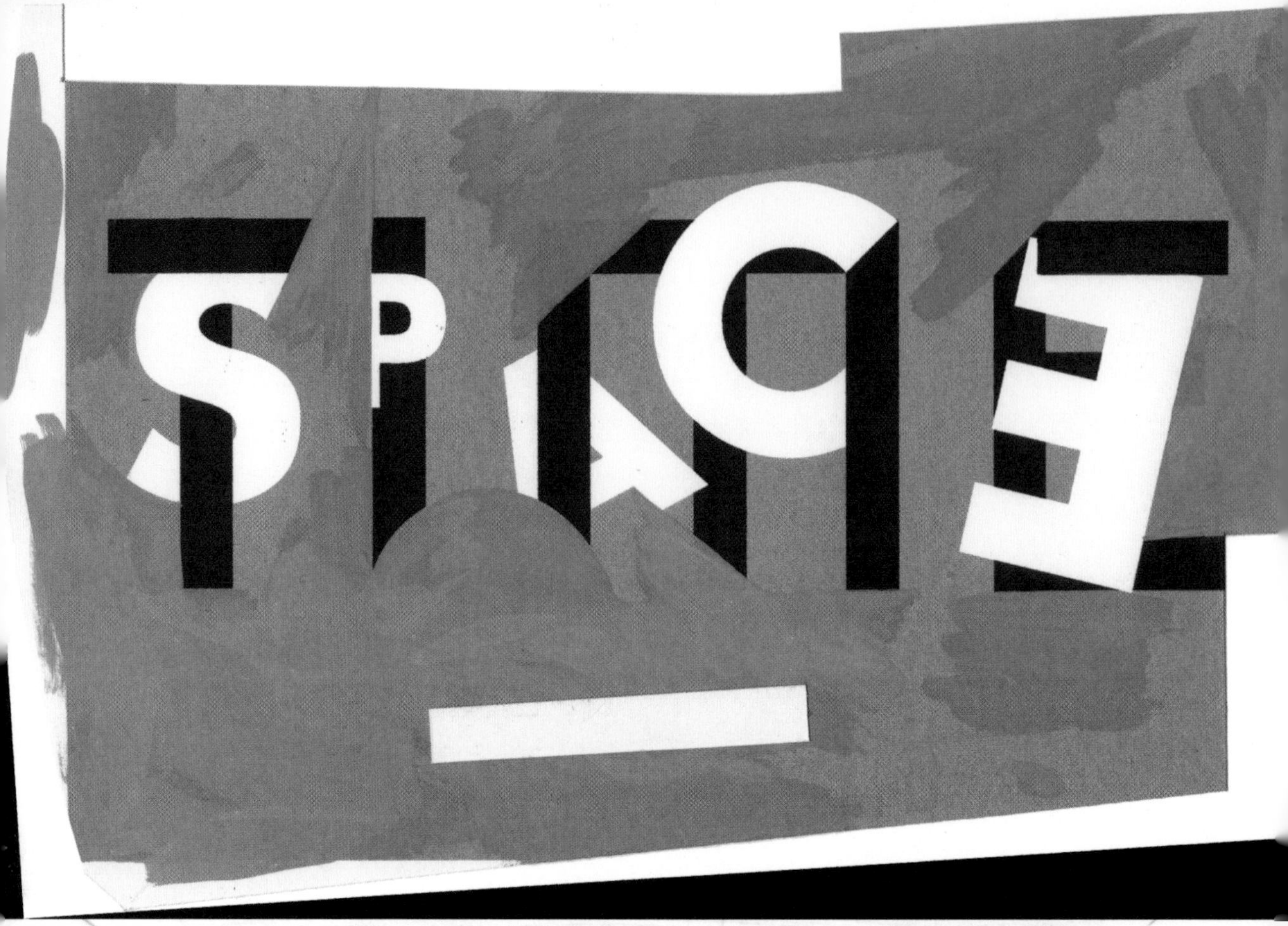
SPACE

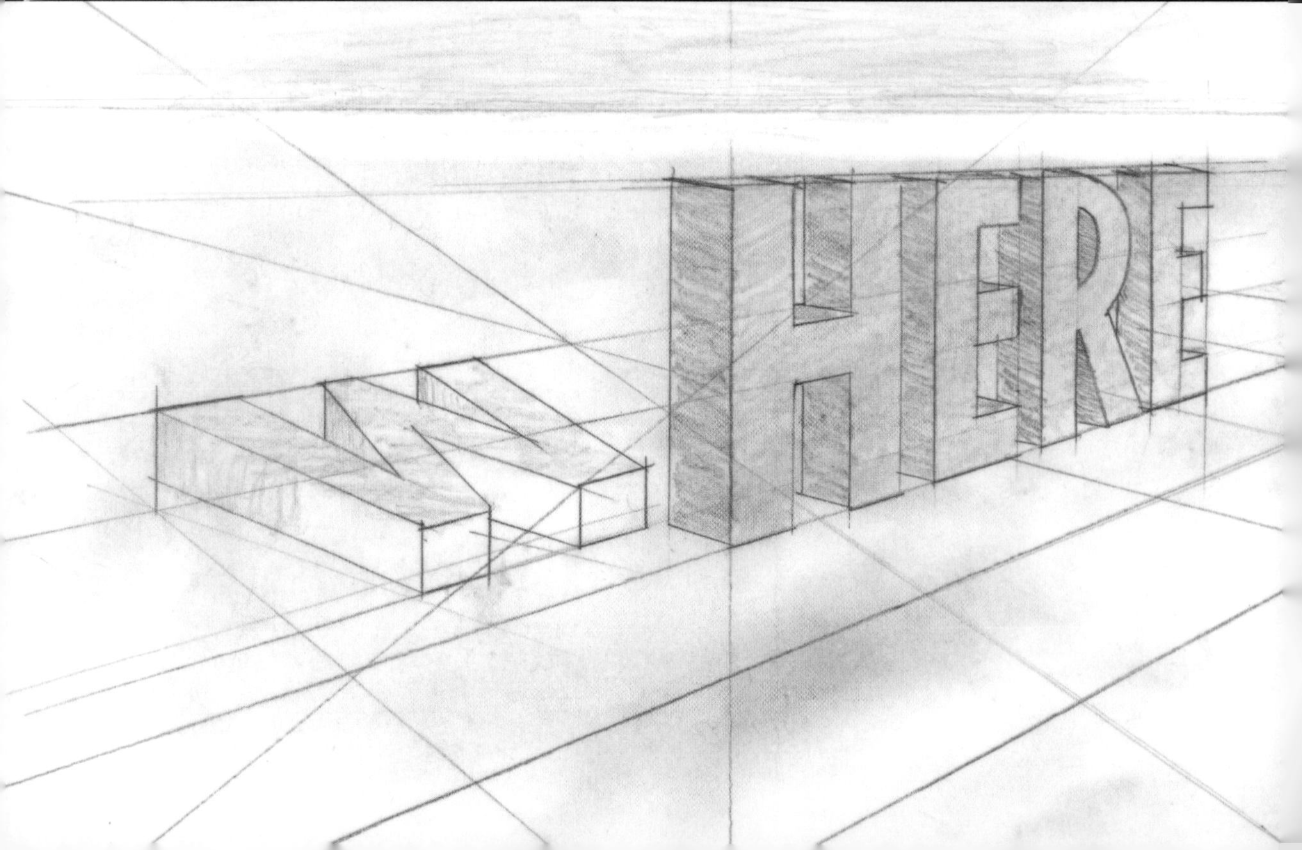
HERE

HiTS

Brush oil 4.08

ALUMINUM LETTERS

IGNORE THIS THOUGHT

pidgeon shit

Toshi Omagari

London · UK

Japanese designer Toshi Omagari creates letterforms for all kinds of writing systems, from Greek to Mongolian – but not Japanese.

'Each writing system deserves more than just a readable font,' he says. 'There has to be some fun with the letters, too. I make two kinds of sketches, one for getting the job done, and the other just for the sake of drawing. I tend to work on existing typefaces that do not require a lot of sketching, and I sketch more for fun.'

Sketches for work are drawn to test the idea and to save time, rather than for quality. The sketched letters and the end results are the same in principle, but are generally vastly improved in their final form.

'With a font editor, the only drawing tool available is Bézier curve, which is too slow and accurate for getting quick ideas,' Toshi says. 'The best part about sketching is the freedom – you can use a variety of tools and colours. I use two mechanical pencils, with different lead thicknesses. I do not fill the outlines with pencils very often, since I always carry a sketchbook and the sketch gets smudged. I either do not fill at all, or fill with ink using two pens – one for outline and the other for fill.'

Toshi uses paper that can withstand repeated eraser rubbings: the texture should not be smooth, but not too soft. 'I always buy sketchbooks when I go to Japan,' he says. 'There is one that I have been a fan of for 12 years.'

01

247

Falcon Punch

Falcon Punch

249

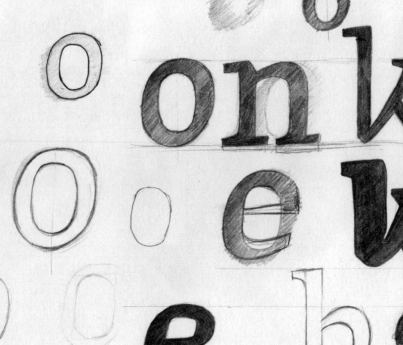

Slávka Pauliková

Amsterdam · Netherlands

Sketching is an important part of graphic designer Slávka Pauliková's creative process. 'Mostly I sketch to get that first idea of what I will be digitizing later, or a sense of how can I work with the design and what my options are,' she explains. 'Usually the finished work looks much different from the sketches.'

Of course, pragmatism also comes into it. 'Sketching gives you faster feedback and lets you explore more options in a shorter amount of time,' Slávka says. 'I do not have a favourite tool, and use a variety for sketching, from all kinds of pencils and brushes to the computer or my phone. Most of the time I sketch on blank sheets of paper.'

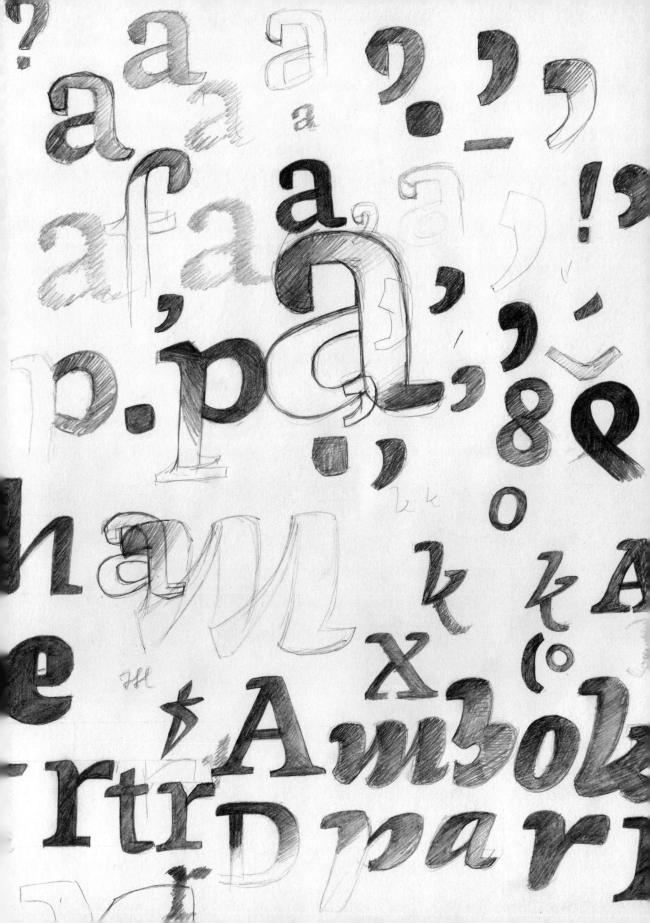

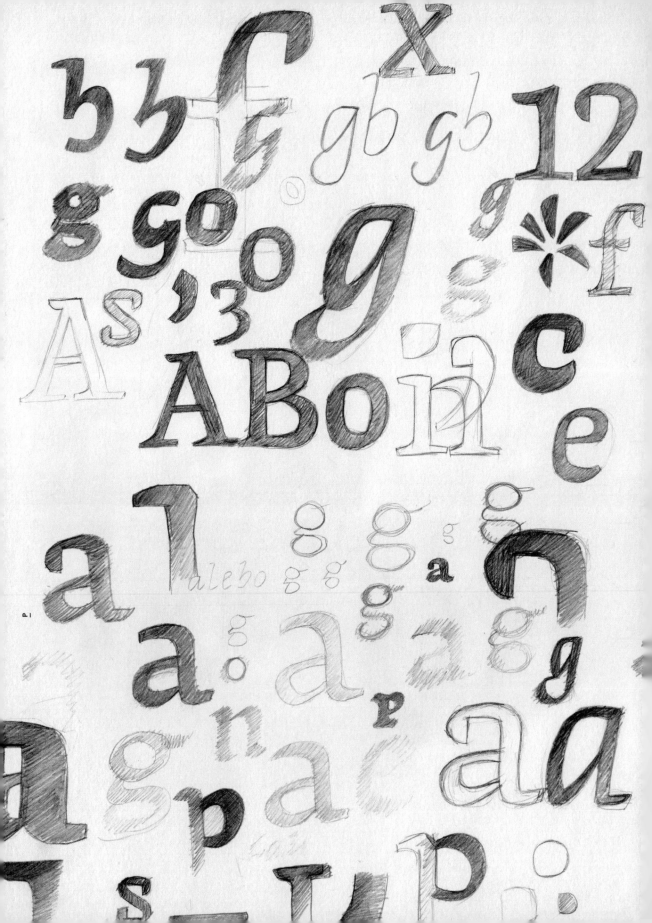

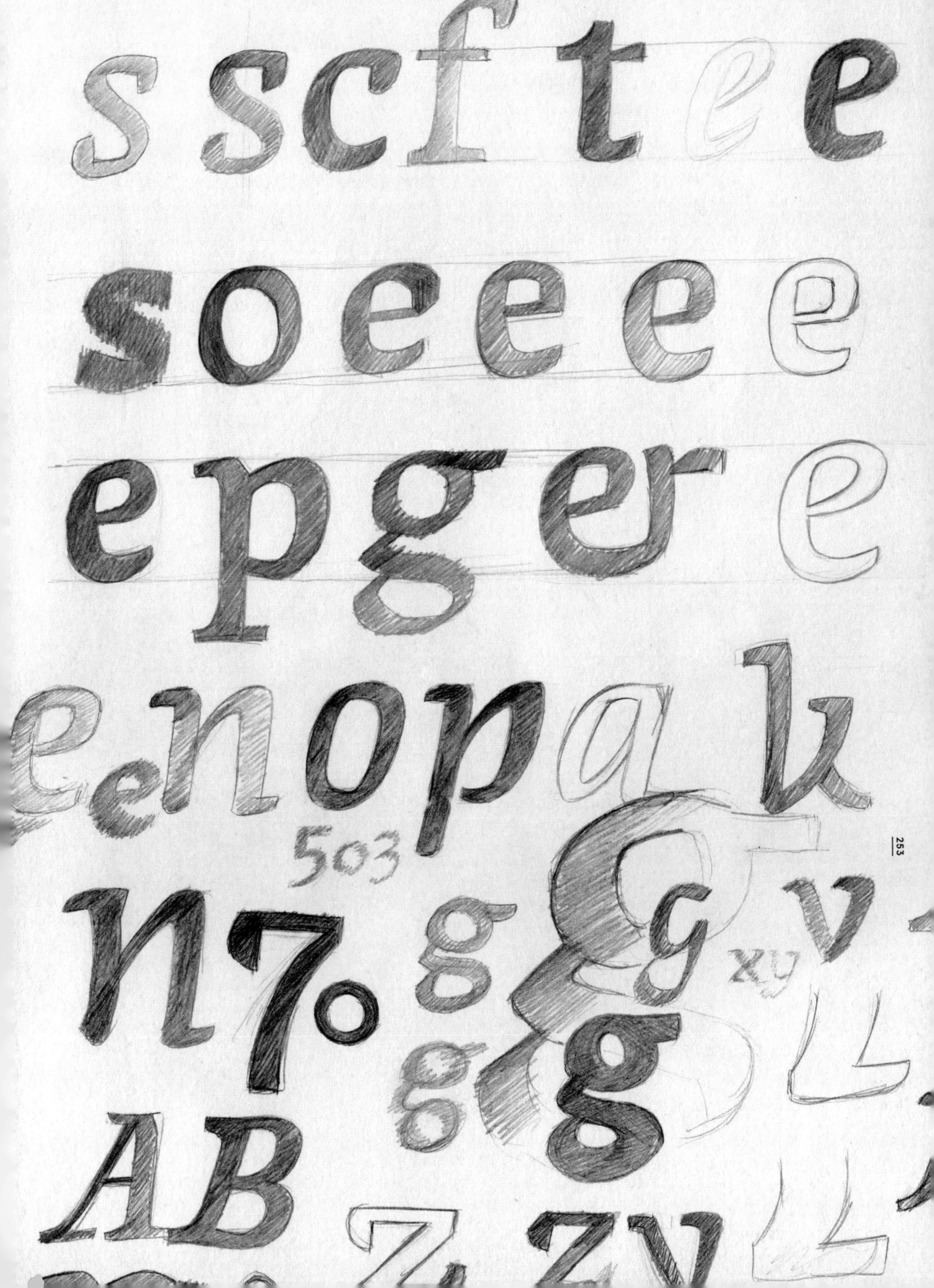

s s c f t e e

s o e e e e e

e p g e e

e n o p a b

503

n 7 o g g g v

g

g

xy

A B

Z z

Judith Poirier

Montreal • Canada

'If we expand the definition of sketch to an unfinished version of a creative work,' says typographic filmmaker Judith Poirier, 'then I can say that there are several phases of sketches involved in making my films. I usually begin by writing ideas on paper, to empty my brain, maybe with a few drawings, but it usually turns out to be lists of things I want to experiment with and production notes.'

Next, she says, 'I begin printing directly onto clear film stock with letterpress, and have short digital transfers made to test ideas for movement and sound. This exploration phase is essential in visualizing a project and to plan the production to come.

The sketches can even serve to assist in the financing of a project, acting as support for a funding application.'

Judith's work is all about experimentation. 'I put the ingredients together, which brings an element of surprise to the pre-sketched ideas,' she says. 'This leads to more ideas, until I have exhausted all possibilities. I love the printed strips of celluloid, as well as discovering the sound produced by the ink on the optical soundtrack area.'

She notes that she does not have the discipline to regularly use a sketchbook. 'I have started several for different projects,' Judith admits, 'but I always end up sketching on a piece of paper here and there.' Eventually, she transfers her sketches into one book: 'I find it useful to have everything in the same place, especially the technical notes, as my projects are often spread out over several years.'

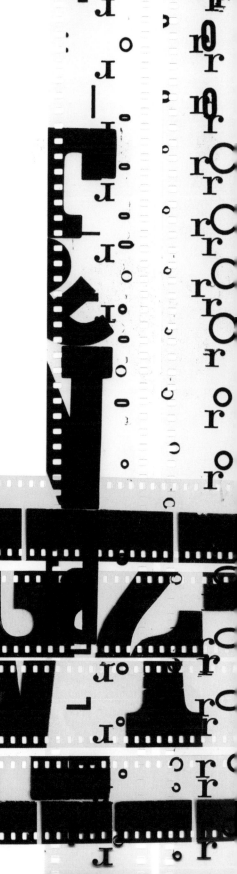

POW!POW!POW! POW

BANK BAN

Carolyn Porter

St Paul • Minnesota • USA

Carolyn Porter often draws letters when she travels, but whether she begins a project with a sketch or not very much depends on the project. 'If I have a clear vision, I might go directly to the computer,' she says. 'But if I only have a concept, I'll sketch. Sketching allows for serendipity in a way that working on the computer doesn't. An unintended curve or an irregular line can turn into a delightful surprise, which will find its way into the final work.'

Carolyn's favourite part of the process is the freedom that sketching gives to explore and make mistakes. 'If something isn't right, I can toss it and start over, or take whatever tiny fragment I love and explore it further,' she explains. 'Perfection isn't expected in sketches.'

Her two go-to tools are a Pentel mechanical pencil and a Rollerball pen with a micro-point. 'I really should pull out the paint and brushes more often,' she admits. 'Years ago, I sketched directly into a sketchbook, but I found the bulky binding was a hindrance to rotating the page to sketch at an angle, sideways or upside down. Now I often sketch on whatever piece of paper is nearby – sometimes it's no more than a scrap – then tape the drawing into the sketchbook.'

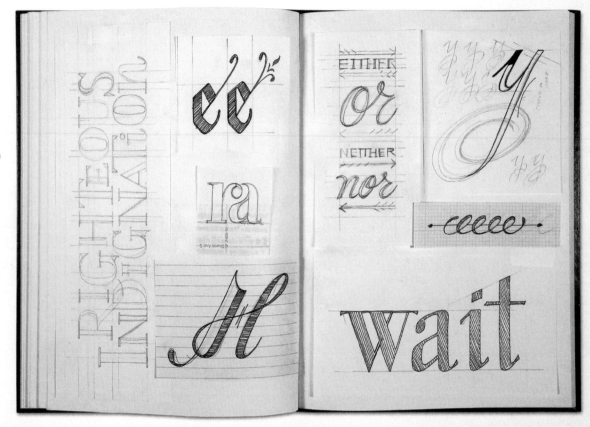

NO SERIF

CARVED IN WOOD @
STOUTS ISLAND LODGE – ENTRYWAY GREETING

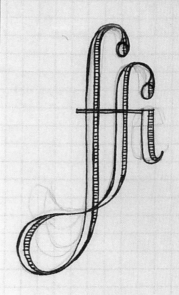

Dan Reisinger
Givatayim · Israel

'Sketching is a continuous dialogue I conduct with myself,' says poster designer Dan Reisinger. Ever since his student days, sketching has been an 'educational tool for improving drawing skills. The need to record ideas is an integral part of my life and work.'

For Dan, the sketching process can be broken down into three categories:

1. Fun. 'The fact that I don't have to do it is what I like most,' he says. 'Sketching opens possibilities, and quite a few drawings become relevant later as design solutions.'

2. Process. When trying to come up with an idea for an assignment, Dan says, 'I will take a sheet of paper and sketch anything that comes to mind. I particularly enjoy the surprise of discovery during this phase. Some of these preliminary sketches end up as final pieces.'

3. Artwork. 'When an idea has been formulated in my mind,' Dan explains, 'the process of how to best express or define the final design takes over.'

Dan continues: 'I am an obsessive guardian of my sketches and design processes. I have a wide range of these materials, from the first sketch of my first poster-design exercise at Bezalel Academy of Arts and Design (which he attended in 1951) to the 40 colour sketches presenting concepts of supergraphics that were recently acquired by the Centre Georges Pompidou in Paris for its "Colour in Architecture" collection.'

The 'quick, spontaneous activity' of sketching has influenced some of his designs, he says, and 'improved my drawing skill, helped me to efficiently present graphic and 3D ideas to clients and, above all, has been a favourite pastime, a way to create/play for no particular purpose or gain. Sketching has taught me to observe, not just look.'

Dan prefers pens, pencils, brushes, pastels, coloured papers and even a camera. 'The pencil is still my favourite,' he says. 'The tool or technique employed leaves its mark on the final outcome of the sketch, more than a certain style. When at home or in the studio, any white paper or clean surface is OK. When I'm on vacation or outdoors, I always carry a sketchbook.'

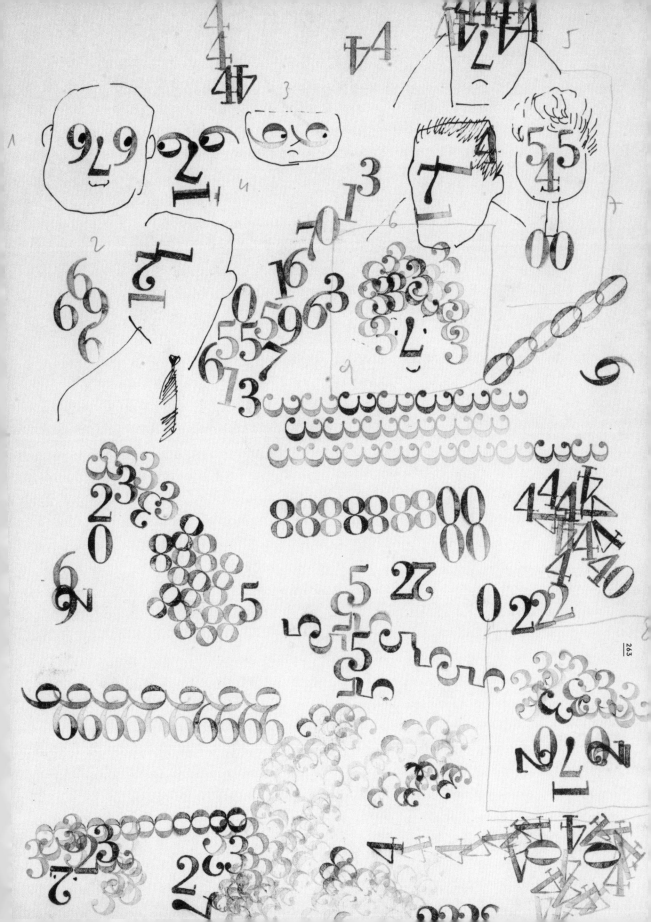

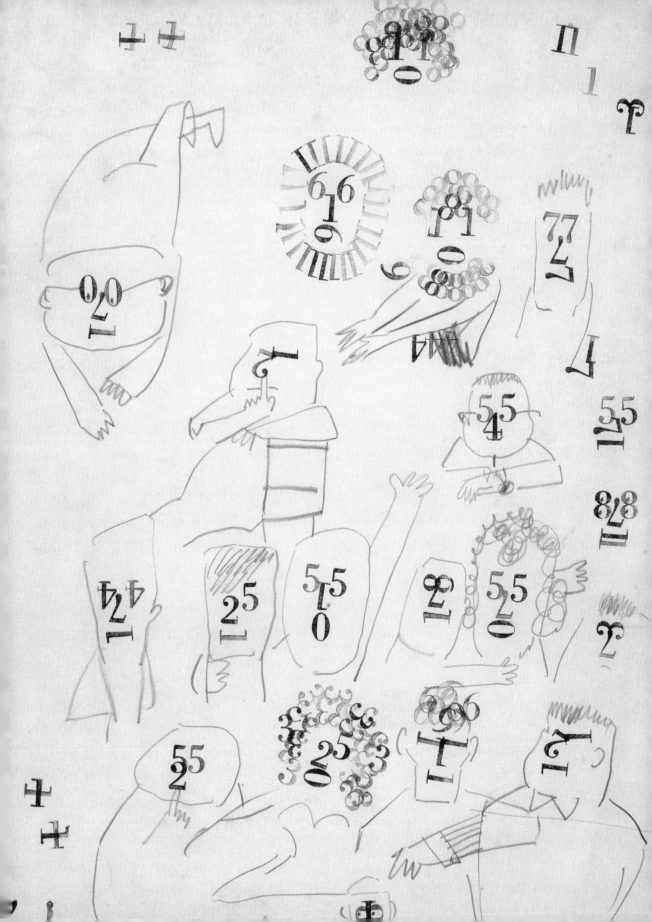

Dan Rhatigan

New York • New York • USA

Sketching is not an essential part of type designer and archivist Dan Rhatigan's routine. 'I really only sketch when I get stuck, can't visualize something properly or have trouble knocking a letter's outlines into shape,' he says.

'When I do sketch,' Dan continues, 'I end up getting more value out of the notes I made about the sketches, so that I could remember what I was trying

to do in the first place. Honestly, I don't like it that much! I get frustrated that I can't draw as well as I'd like, or as well as I once did. I draw details or basic shapes, to capture something so that I don't lose the idea. I admit that sketching is useful, but it's usually linked to a moment of frustration in my thinking.'

The sketching process has a significant impact on those situations when, Dan explains, 'I have to step back and sketch to clarify what I'm thinking, which helps to maintain any looseness or freshness in the end result. My sketches nag me along the way, reminding me what the more natural gesture in a given letter or design may be.'

When Dan does sketch he will use anything that's to hand, but usually a crisp mechanical pencil or a black pen with a small, precise tip. 'I don't really have a feel for working with a brush,' he admits. 'Ironically, brush sketching has got me out of some of my worst ruts. For me, a computer is more about constructing than about sketching.'

When it comes to sketchbooks, however, Dan uses them because it's easier to keep his thoughts organized. 'Also going to a lot of design events leads to a large collection of little blank sketchbooks,' he concludes, 'and I hate to see them go to waste.'

4/12/07

slightly lighter color,
less contrast than Ging

strong horizontal

ɿaa a

slight taper

sharp turn to exaggerate

90°

deep cut

horizontality

ah

slab

slight taper

slight
taper

very horizontal

es

This will need to be
rounder

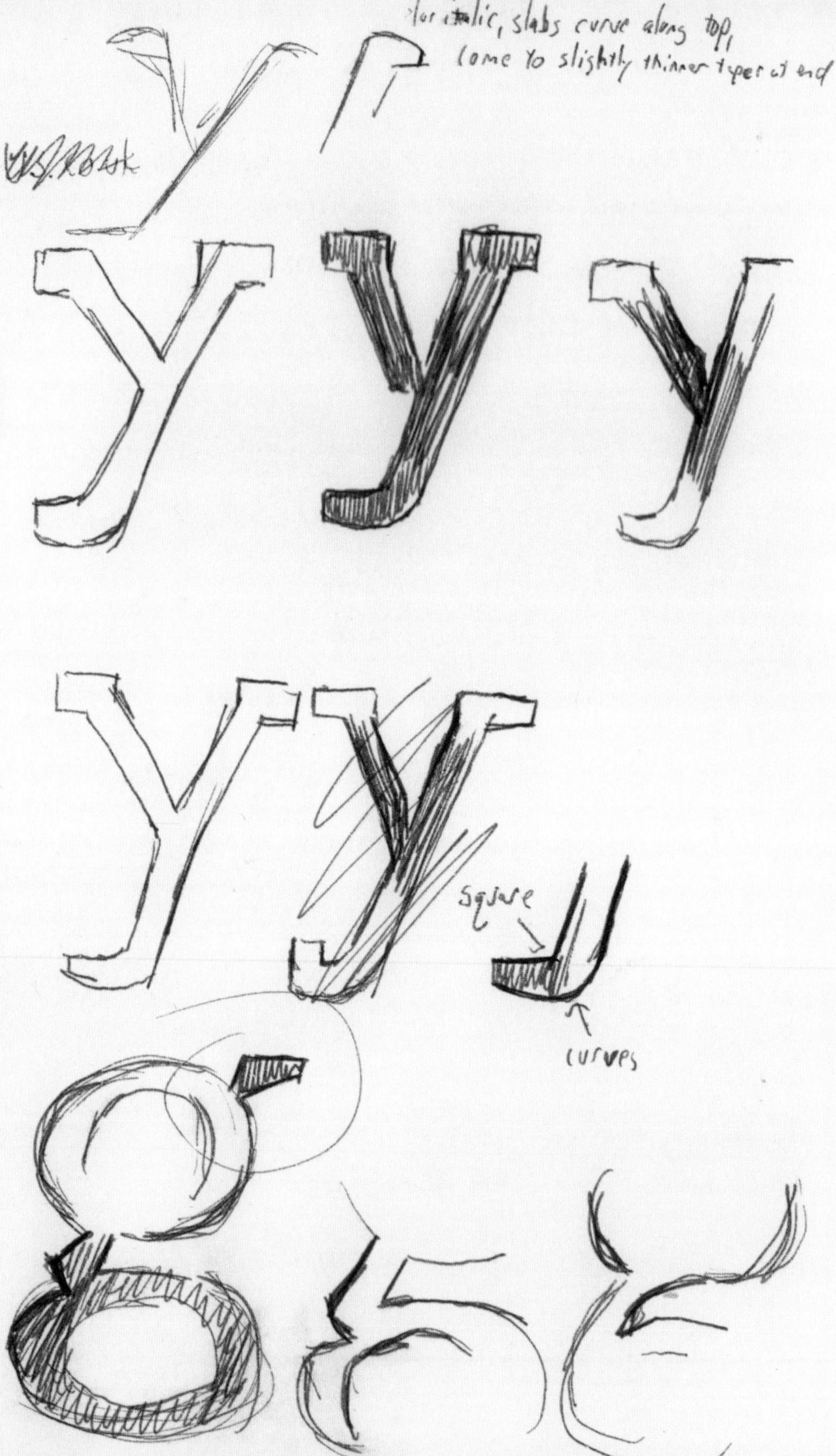

for italic, slabs curve along top,
come to slightly thinner types at end

y y y y

y y

square

curves

8 5 5

R 1

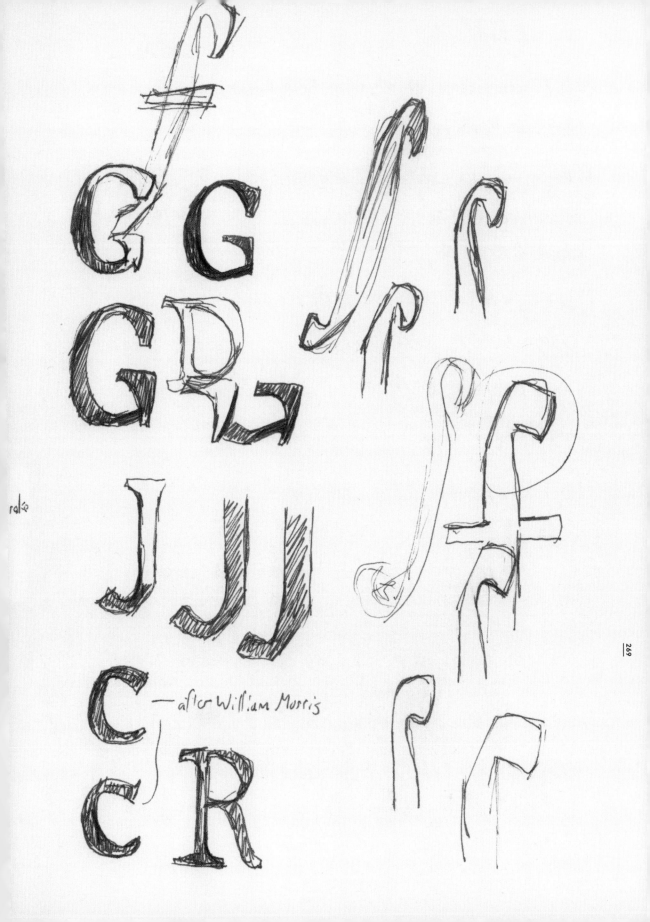

—after William Morris

Bud Rodecker

Chicago • Illinois • USA

Sketching, says Bud Rodecker, principal designer at Thirst and adjunct professor at DePaul University, allows him the freedom to explore the parameters of a project quickly, and to see what is interesting and what isn't. 'It usually allows me to get to the finished design faster,' he continues. 'Once my ideas are on the page, I can judge which of them to explore further.'

Bud uses a Pilot Precise V5 or a Pentel Sign pen and Illustrator or InDesign. For personal projects he uses sketchbooks, but when he is working in the studio, loose sheets of paper work best. 'That way I can sketch how something should look and leave it with the person I'm working with,' he explains. 'When I'm designing something and have moved on to the computer, I use InDesign or Adobe Illustrator documents as if they were pages in a sketchbook. I save versions along the way, until I find the right one.'

Bud designed 'Breast Wishes' (pp. 274–5) for his wife's breast-cancer walk team – which ended up on a T-shirt worn by the team. The 'RicharDaily' type (below and opposite) came out of geometric type experiments for his RicharDaily project in 2010. 'One of the earliest explorations was my attempt to find a more playful version of the geometric type trend I saw at the time,' Bud explains. 'I developed my own vocabulary of geometric letterforms, which can be scaled and stretched into interesting nested combinations.'

The 'YAB' panels (overleaf) were part of a submission to a group show organized by Matthew Hoffman. 'I was given a wooden panel etched with the "You Are Beautiful" motto and asked to apply a graphic to it,' Bud says. 'After sketching the ideas by hand, I made some of them in Illustrator to test them out. In the end, I made two options: 1) I ordered custom fortune cookies that said "in bed" to hand out on the night, and 2) I created a RicharDaily-style type composition that said "Let 'be' be the finale of seem". It seemed like a nice sentiment for the show.'

I AM
THE PEOPLE!
THE CROWD
THE MASS

THE

THANKS! THANKS!

YOU ARE
beautiful

very

MIRROR

LAJAR APP

YOU ARE
XXXXXXX

LENTICULAR

YOU ARE
beautiful

REGULAR   VERY
SPECIAL   MOSTLY
UNIQUE   the
PRETTY   MY
SUCCESSFUL   OUR
FAMOUS   SO
SMART   BECAUSE
INTELLIGENT   SIMPLY
GREAT   REGULAR
FINE   TERRIBLY
OK   SINFULLY
NICE   TYPICALLY
SWEET   HISTORICALLY
OUT OF MY   UNIQUELY
   LEAGUE   ARTFULLY
ACCOMPLISHED   TRADITIONALLY
HERE   UNTRADITIONALLY
PRESENT
STRONG

SAY are?
beautiful!

MOM
beautiful

you are
surprisingly
beautiful

you are
beautiful

you are
beautiful

you are
beautiful

you are
beautiful

you are
beautiful

CARILYN SONMAN

103

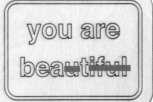

LADY LADY
LUMPS LUMPS

BREAST
WISHES

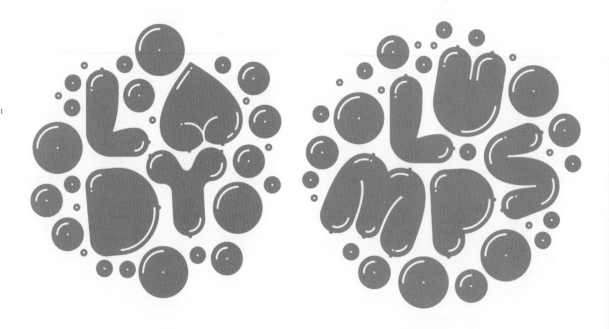

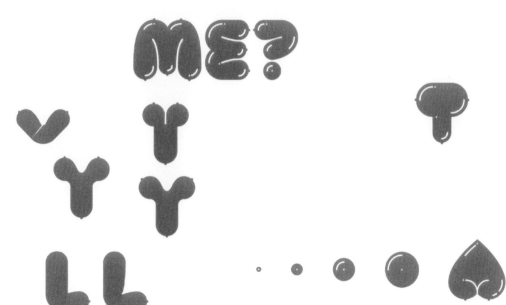

Mamoun Sakkal

Bothell • Washington • USA

'Sketching is an essential part of my work routine, whether I'm designing a typeface or a logo,' says Syrian artist and calligrapher Mamoun Sakkal. 'It is an efficient way of making explorations into new ideas, and then refining those ideas that seem the most promising or exciting.'

Pencils have been gradually replaced with pens, and pens with sketching on computers. 'I still use all of these, as well as occasionally reed pens and brushes,' he says. 'I also find myself often using sketches to create new designs on the computer by revising digitally or creating new compositions.'

Mamoun continues: 'I rarely go back and review these sketches when working on new typefaces, because each time my sketching is focused on solving a specific problem or exploring images within certain visual parameters.'

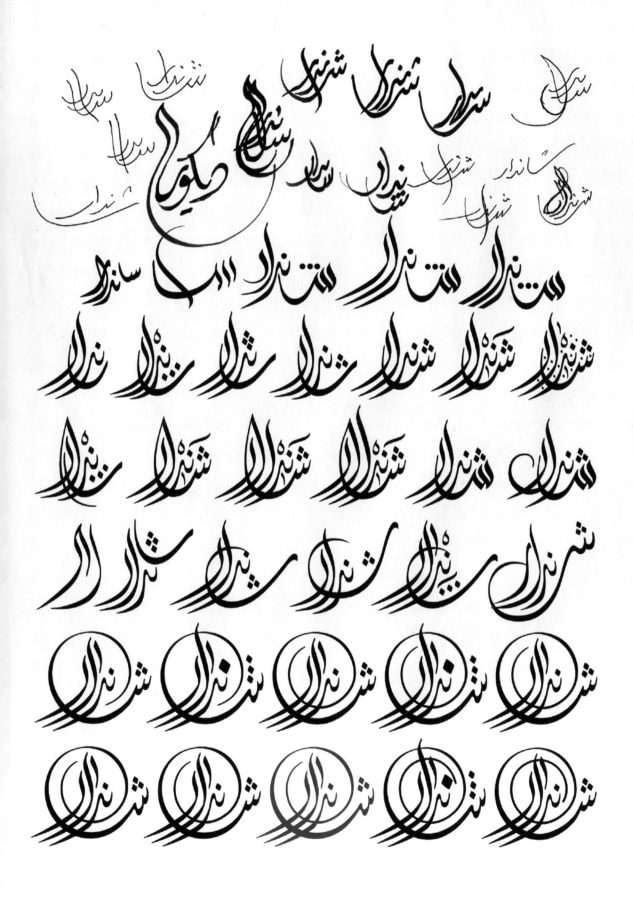

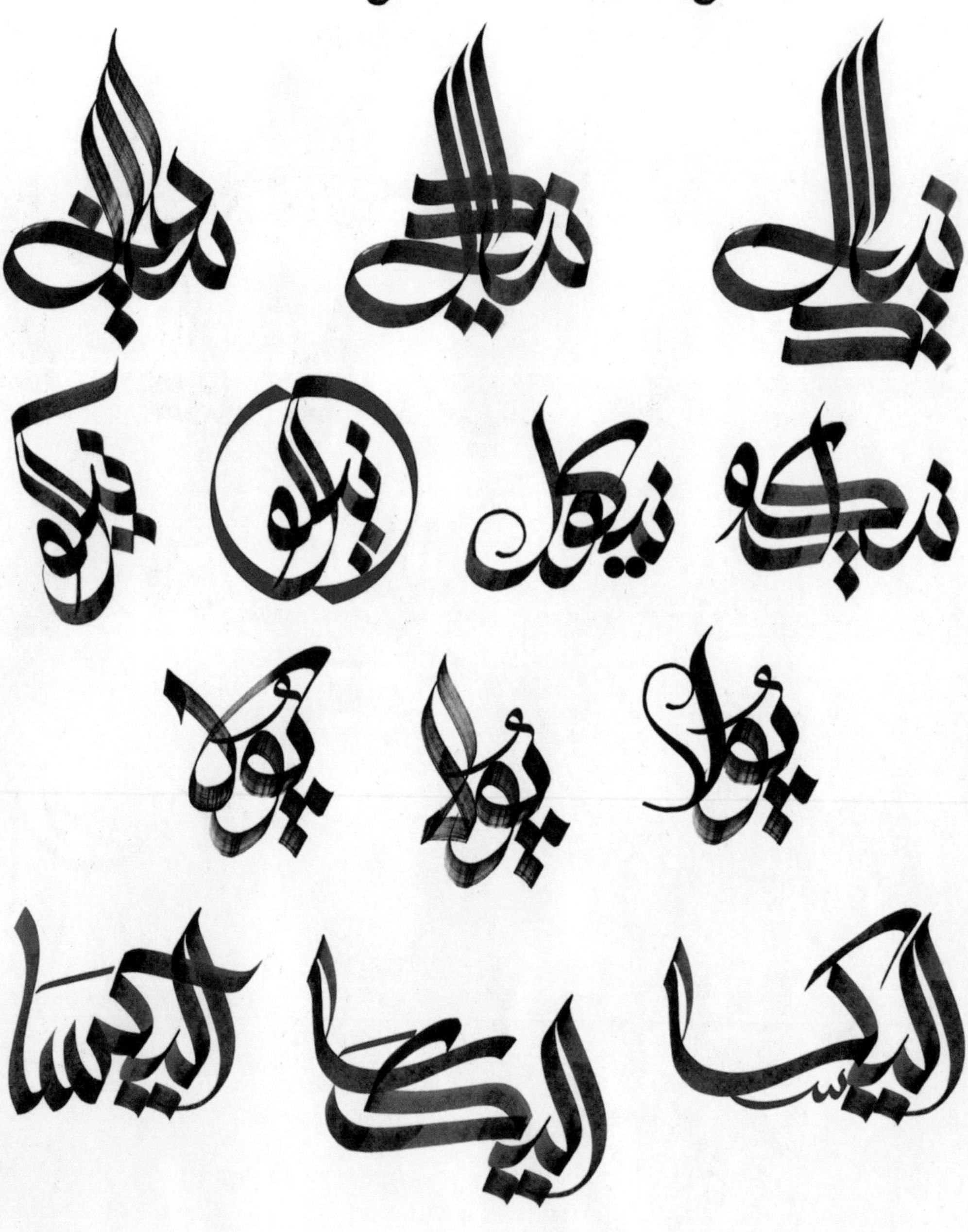

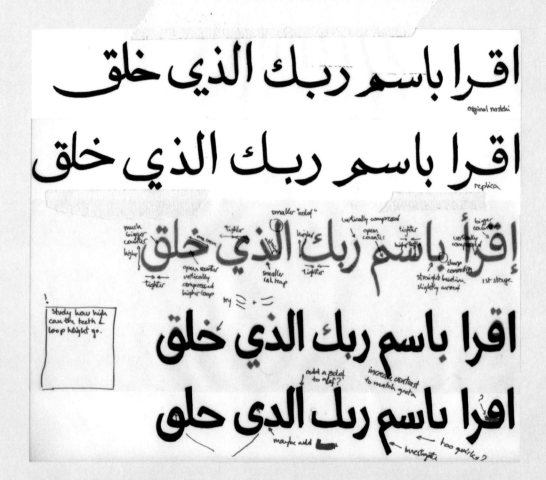

Kristyan Sarkis

The Hague • Netherlands

'At every part of the process, especially the beginning, sketching helps me clear my mind and see ideas concretely,' says Kristyan Sarkis, 'so that I can make better decisions about what to build on and how to proceed.'

Sketching, especially by hand, enables him to spend more time with the letterforms and better understand the tiniest details. 'It also allows you to think visually of different ways of experimenting,' he says, 'changing the tools, technique, materials, and so on.'

Most of his sketches are made in his sketchbooks, but there are also what Kristyan calls his 'calligraphic sketches'. These are, he explains, 'essentially calligraphy exercises, to manipulate letterforms and extract their different characteristics. They are normally made on large sheets of paper with layers of tracing paper. Occasionally,

I practise on smooth coated paper for a better glide of the pens.'

Kristyan recalls his first meeting with type designer Gerrit Noordzij in 2010: 'When he walked into our classroom my Thuraya sketches were among the first things he saw. He asked, "So, in Arabic you have thick overlapping strokes?" When I said yes, reluctantly, he replied, "Fantastic!" That started a conversation about how we could begin dealing with such an issue. I can clearly remember thinking, "we have a long way to go with Arabic letterforms in digital type!"'

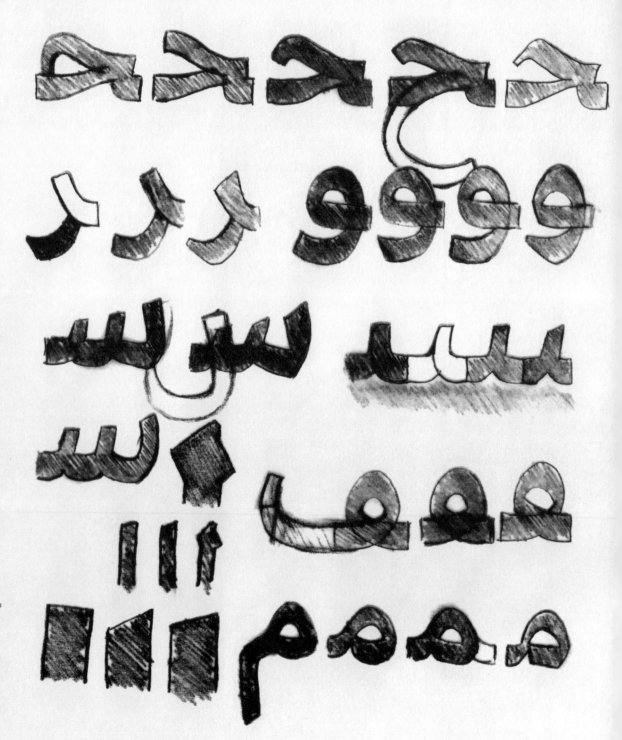

ا ر ا وحب قالت

م حہ سہ د

الپیر ر ر

مد مد مم مم

و و ح ح

د ح ح د

د ر ر

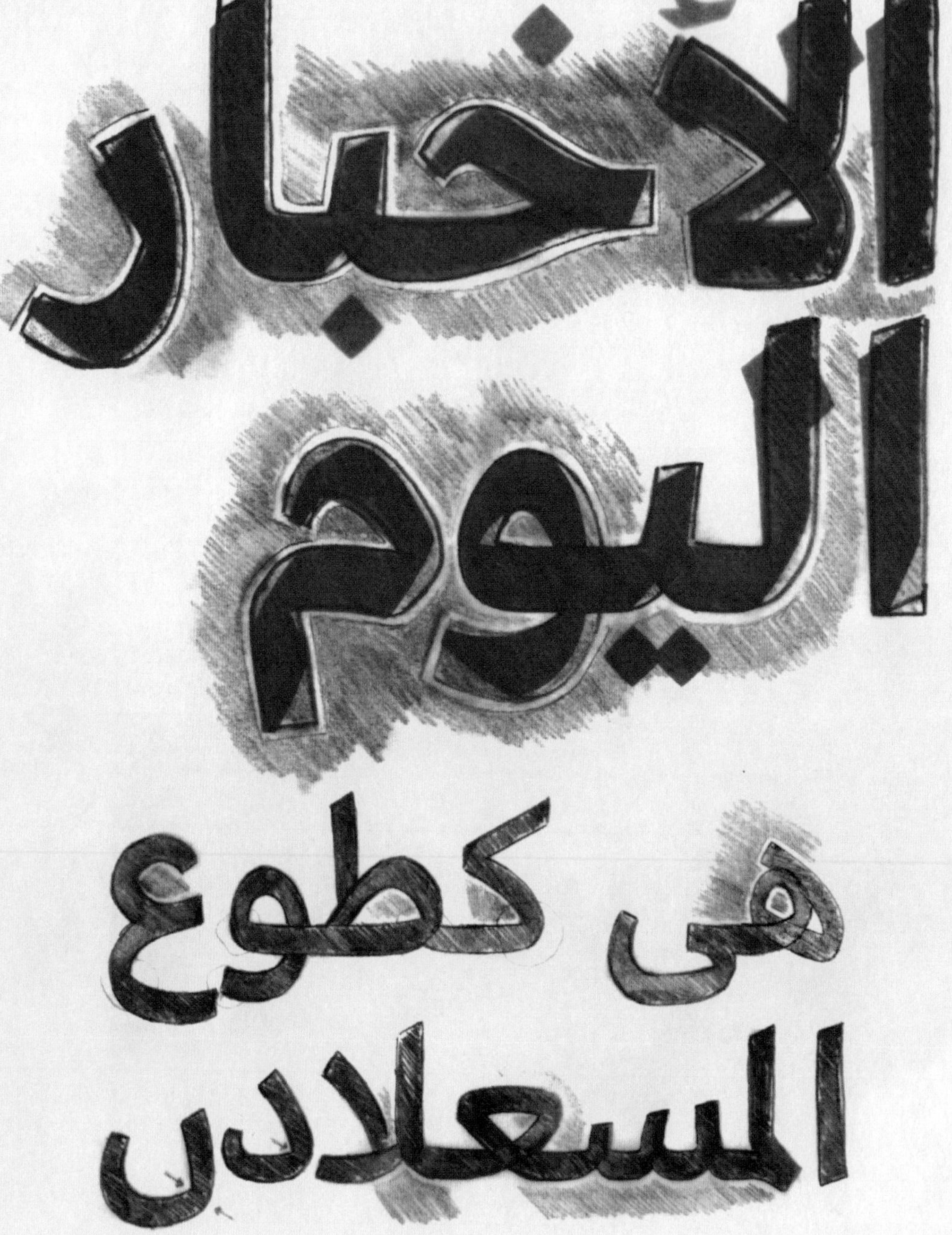
الأخبار
اليوم
هى كطوع
المسعلادن

285

Little Plane
LEARNS TO WRITE

LEDYARD

Stephen Savage

Brooklyn · New York · USA

Illustrator and children's book author Stephen Savage has a pocket sketchbook on him at all times. 'Sketching helps to distil a visual idea,' he says. 'Tom Woodruff, my MFA professor at the School of Visual Arts, once told me that if a drawing works on a cocktail napkin, it will work as a final illustration. Sage advice.'

Stephen works mostly on conceptual or narrative illustrations, but lettering often plays a role. Sketching, he says, is 'quick and direct, and a refreshing change from my digital routine'. These days, he works mainly with mechanical pencils and black felt-tip markers. 'I prefer sketchbooks,' he says, 'but I also like drawing on the paper placemats in restaurants. My seven-year-old daughter and I fight over the crayons.'

What is Stephen's favourite sketchbook anecdote? 'A few summers ago, I stayed at a beach house in Rhode Island with my family. I spent the mornings sitting in an Adirondack chair on the porch, drawing and painting in a spiral-bound sketchbook. One afternoon, there was a huge thunderstorm and everything on the porch, including the sketchbook, got wet. The pages were completely soaked, but somehow the ink and watercolours did not run. I spent the last week of our holiday drying each page out on a clothesline. I call it my "miracle" sketchbook.'

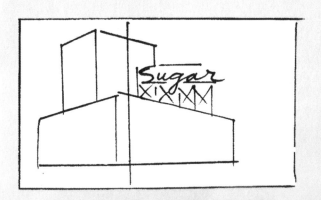

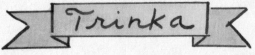

Flag guy works on
the ground floor of the
building.

He wishes he could
work at the top.

They'd notice
if I worked
at the top!

So he started to climb.
starts

But he didn't get far.
(very high)

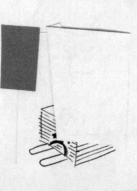

Then, he climbed jumped aboard
a fork lift.

(Still, he didn't get
very high.) But that
didn't get him very
high either.

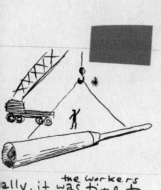

Finally, it was time to
hoist the spire on to
the very top of the
building. This was
Flag Guy's last chance.
He climbed inside.

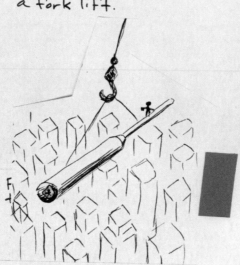

The Spire climbs
higher and higher.
Flag guy walks out
to the tip. ~~XXXXXXXXXX~~
He can see the
whole city!

Suddenly, the
spire is hoisted
into place.
Flag Guy slips off.

He floated back down...
He gets back down safely.

...without his flag.
But he's missing his flag.

But then EVERYBODY
saw it.
sees

At the
very top!

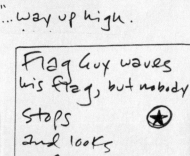

"...way up high.

"...re it is"!

Everybody in town saw it.

The skyscraper...

Flag Guy waves
his flag, but nobody
stops   ⭐
and looks
and smiles
What would it be like
to work up HIGH?

And they all stopped.

p!", cries
g Guy. But
dy stops.
ody notices

Oh, how he wishes he
could work up high
above the street.

But what he really
wants to do is build!

The School children
saw it.

...t to work
the top," he thinks.

Crane

Then,
Everybody looked up.

They all knew.

Bijan
Sayfouri

Tehran • Iran

Graphic designer Bijan Sayfouri spent his childhood and adolescence in Iran's western border cities during the revolution and ensuing war. His earliest works were published in 1978, when he was 10 years old. In high school, he began making his first stencilled posters, applying them to the city walls of Sanandaj, the capital of Kurdistan Province, and, after studying at the School of Fine Arts at Tehran University, set up his own studio in Tehran in 1988.

Bijan is known for his expressive and conceptual approach, and sketching out these ideas has been a significant part of his design process. In 2006 Bijan, along with 55 artists from around the world, was invited to participate in the Remastered project in San Francisco, California, which set out to recreate some of the world's most important masterpieces. He has been on the editorial board of the Italian Design Association since 2010, and established the MeFoundation, based in Milan, serving as its art director.

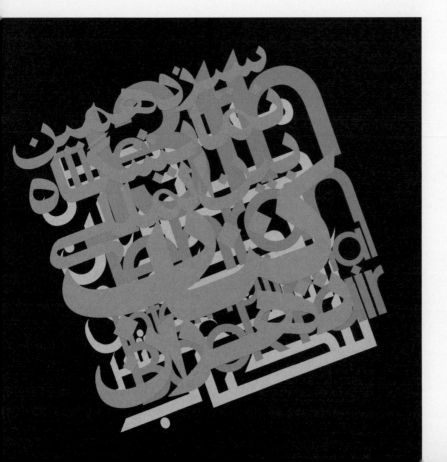

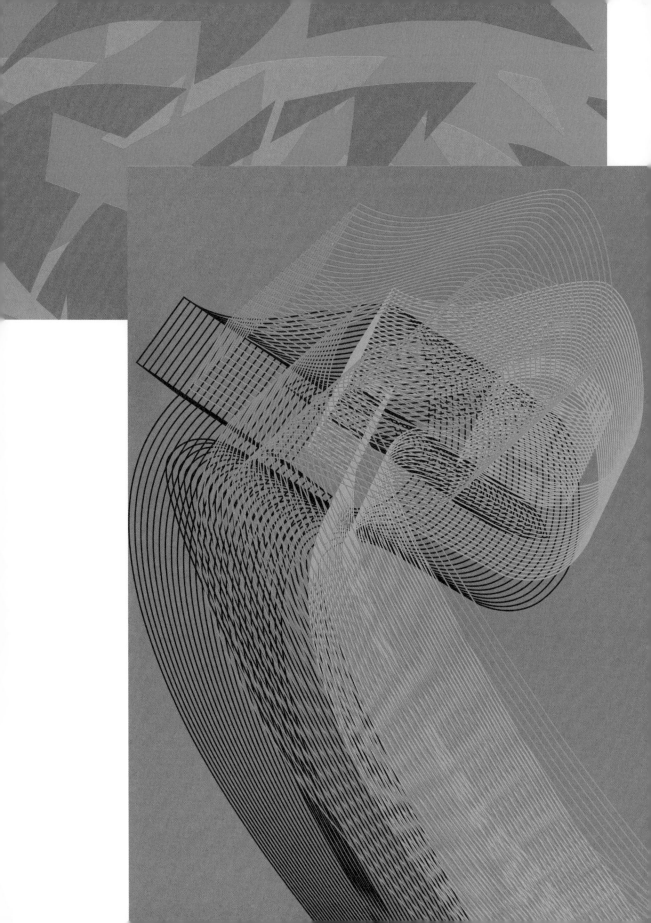

Jeff Scher

Westport • Connecticut • USA

'Sketching is everything I can't do in my head,' says filmmaker and graphic artist Jeff Scher. 'I need the reactive and exploratory loop of hand-eye-brain. I can start drawing with only the vaguest of ideas, but seeing what develops on paper gives a direction.'

In his animated film work, sketching often reveals 'textures and flavours of lines that are essential to the final product,' Jeff explains. 'This is especially true when the final work is handmade.' The best thing about sketching, he continues, is the freedom that 'there is no right or wrong, just the white of the paper egging you on. You can explore hopeless ideas to determine if they are indeed hopeless, or harbouring some germ of brilliance.'

A master drawer and film editor uses anything that will make a mark on paper. 'Whatever is handy is good,' Jeff says. 'I pretty much always have my favourite pen of the moment in my shirt pocket, so most likely that's what I'm going to use. I am particularly fond of black felt-tip calligraphy pens with the widest possible tips. You can adjust the line weight wildly, from a thread to a road stripe.'

Sketchbooks increase Jeff's chance of finding ideas later, when he wants to go back and revisit them. 'The good thing about a sketchbook is that you can always turn a page to start fresh, and when you close it, it's put away. Loose bits of paper go straight in the recycling bin or the collage box.'

And his motto for drawing? 'Water really is the universal solvent!'

Jeffrey No yes

L'eau Life

l'eau

l'eau

milk of amnesia

Zachary Quinn Scheuren

Tokyo • Japan

Zachary Quinn Scheuren, a script specialist at Monotype who has mastered the art of Khmer calligraphy and type, does not sketch perfect letters to then be transferred to the computer.

For Zachary, sketching is more about exploration and experimentation, so while it influences what goes into the computer, designs and ideas don't necessarily remain the same from one stage to the next. 'Sketching helps me visualize abstract ideas, even if I don't touch the paper,' he says. 'Just taking a pencil to a blank page and moving my hand around will get my mind working on solving problems and figuring out solutions. It's also a nice, peaceful activity that can be done anywhere, at any time, which is relaxing.'

Zachary is most comfortable with using pencils, calligraphy pens and brushes, usually in formal sketchbooks, but sometimes, he admits, 'the feeling strikes when loose sheets of paper are at hand'.

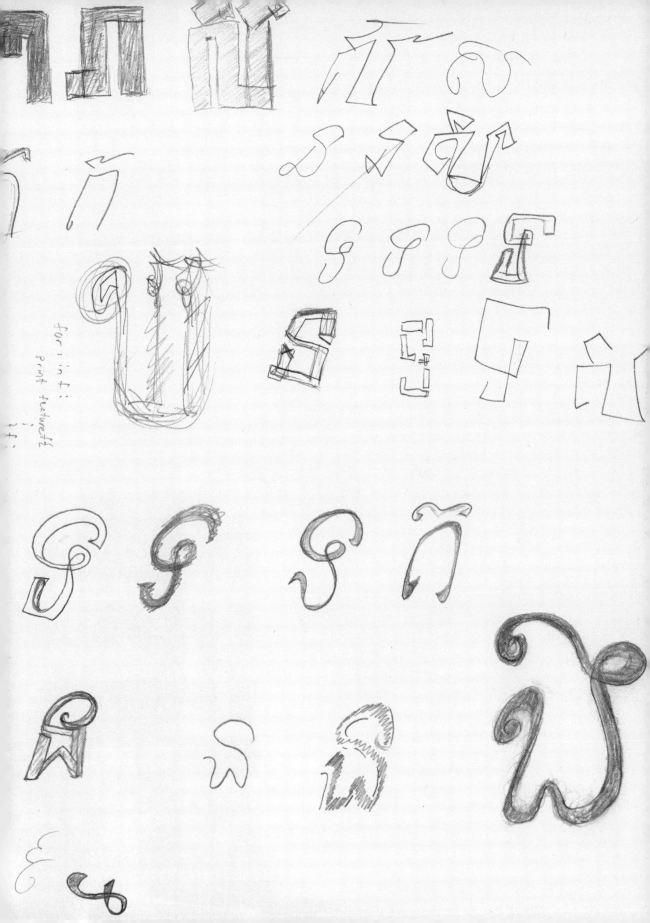

for int:
print feature?
;
2f.

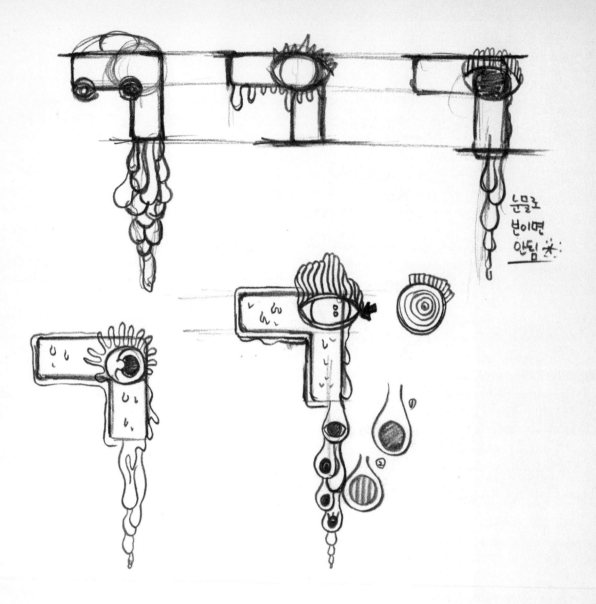

Goeun Seo

New York • New York • USA

The process of sketching makes the work of artist and illustrator Goeun Seo deeper and richer. 'I can add details in various ways,' she says. 'Sketching helps me go in the right direction. If I go too far, I can always look back at what I had at the first stage. Because I'm aware of where I am, it helps me stay in balance.'

Goeun continues: 'I don't need to think very carefully. I can be relaxed and draw naturally, possibly making a few mistakes.' She prefers to mix pens, pencils and brushes while drawing: 'I like pencils, because they have a more natural feeling, and I can draw on the top of an original image I drew earlier and erase easily. Pens and brushes can make different thicknesses and shapes, so I can bring out the liveliness of the sketches.'

Goeun works on any clean surface, whether in notebooks or on random scraps of paper. 'I keep all of them in the one plastic file, because I don't want to lose anything,' she says. For one experiment, she drew letters that looked more like scenes from a horror film. She admits that they don't look much like letters, but they are: 'I kept trying to draw eyes, noses and legs and mix them together. I made my typefaces look like figures – kind of adorable, but with emotion. People couldn't imagine it, yet they loved it. It was fun to surprise them.'

라학 ㅋ 내부구조

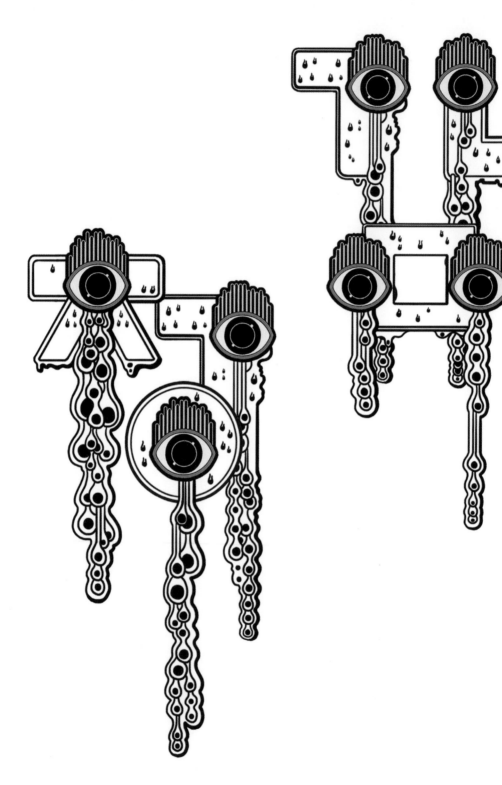

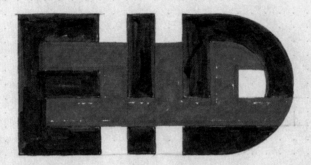

Mohammad Sharaf

New York • New York • USA

Sketching is essential to Kuwaiti designer Mohammad Sharaf's thought process, 'from forming the shape at the beginning of a project to the refinement of the final work'. He continues: 'Sketching has taught me to look closer and pay attention to details, and to trust my eyes more than the data I get from a set of grids and numbers.'

Mohammad tends to use pencils at the early design stage. Inking comes later, when he begins to see the potential in one form, and begins sketching digitally. Later still, he will work on all of these types of sketching simultaneously. 'When it comes to typography and letterforms,' he says, 'I tend to spend most of the time sketching on paper with pencils and pens. I like sketchbooks with grids,' he explains, 'because I usually start sketching letterforms, or words using the Square Kufic, which illustrate a very basic form of Arabic letters.

Of the 'Eid' sketch (above and opposite), he says: 'I design digital greetings for posting onto social media. One year when Eid al-Fitr (a day of celebration that follows Ramadan) was approaching, I was extremely busy with a type-design workshop at the University of Reading in the UK, so I decided not to design a greeting post that year.'

Later on, he continues, 'I found the English word "Eid" in white, over a fairly dark image. The first thing that caught my attention was the negative space, and I began imagining what it would be like to fit the Arabic word for Eid in that space. I drew what I imagined in my sketchbook right away. The English and Arabic fit together perfectly! I took a photo, transferred it to my laptop, digitized it and had a greeting illustration, ready to go.'

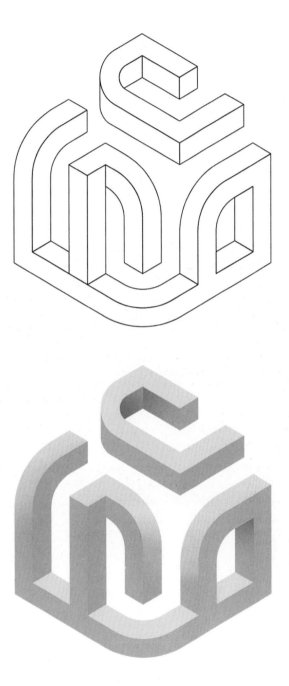

Mark Simonson

St Paul · Minnesota · USA

'Sketching often happens during idle moments, when I draw letters in a stream-of-consciousness way,' says type designer Mark Simonson.

As a rule, he does not trace directly from his sketches: 'They are more like notes, a way of getting an idea out of my head and onto paper so that I will remember it. Sometimes I do tighter sketches that I trace on the computer, but I find it faster if I skip that stage.'

It is the connection between eye, brain and hand that appeals to Mark. 'It feels natural,' he says, 'although that may just be because it's how I started. If I had started out using a mouse, perhaps sketching with a pencil would feel unnatural. There's something so simple and direct about it: you just need a pencil or pen, a sheet of paper and your imagination.'

His tools are mostly pens, especially fine felt-tip ones, or occasionally a Rollerball. Sharpies may be fun to draw with, but they bleed. 'Computers have been a disappointment for sketching,' Mark adds, 'but I think they will get there. I've tried things like Cintiq, but it never feels as good as a pen or pencil.'

About sketchbooks, he says, 'I'm not very organized with them. I tend to use whatever is handy. I like yellow legal pads for some reason, and sometimes I use graph paper. At some point in the last 10 years I got into the habit of putting dates on sketches. I never used to think about that until I had several decades of stuff and attempted to organize it.'

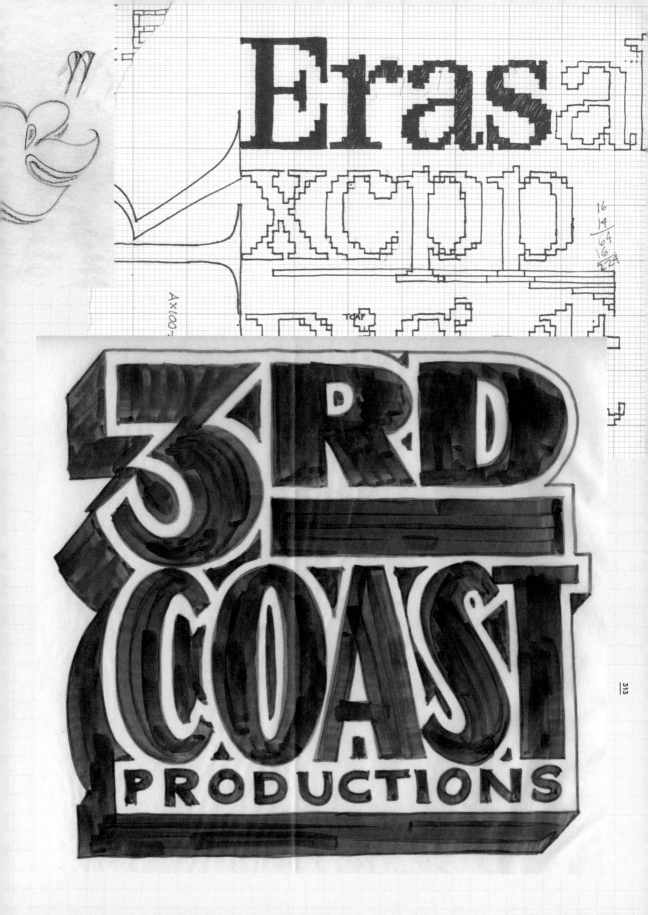

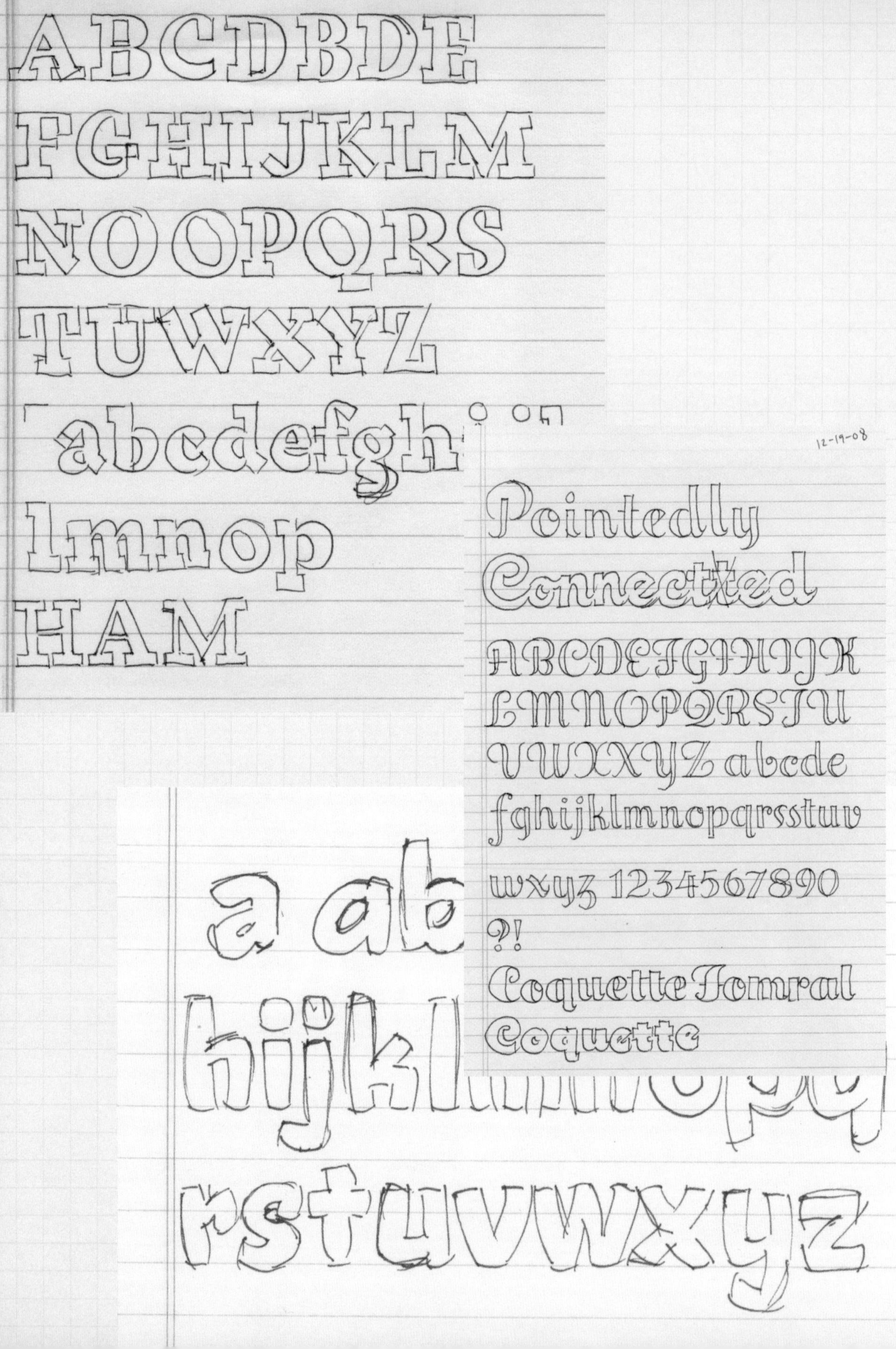

ABCDBDE
FGHIJKLM
NOOPQRS
TUWXYZ
abcdefgh °°⌐
lmnop
HAM

12-19-08

Pointedly
Connectted
ABCDEFGHIJK
LMNOPQRSTU
VWXYZ abcde
fghijklmnopqrsstuv
wxyz 1234567890
?!
Coquette Jomral
Coquette

a ab
hijkl mnopy
rstuvwxyz

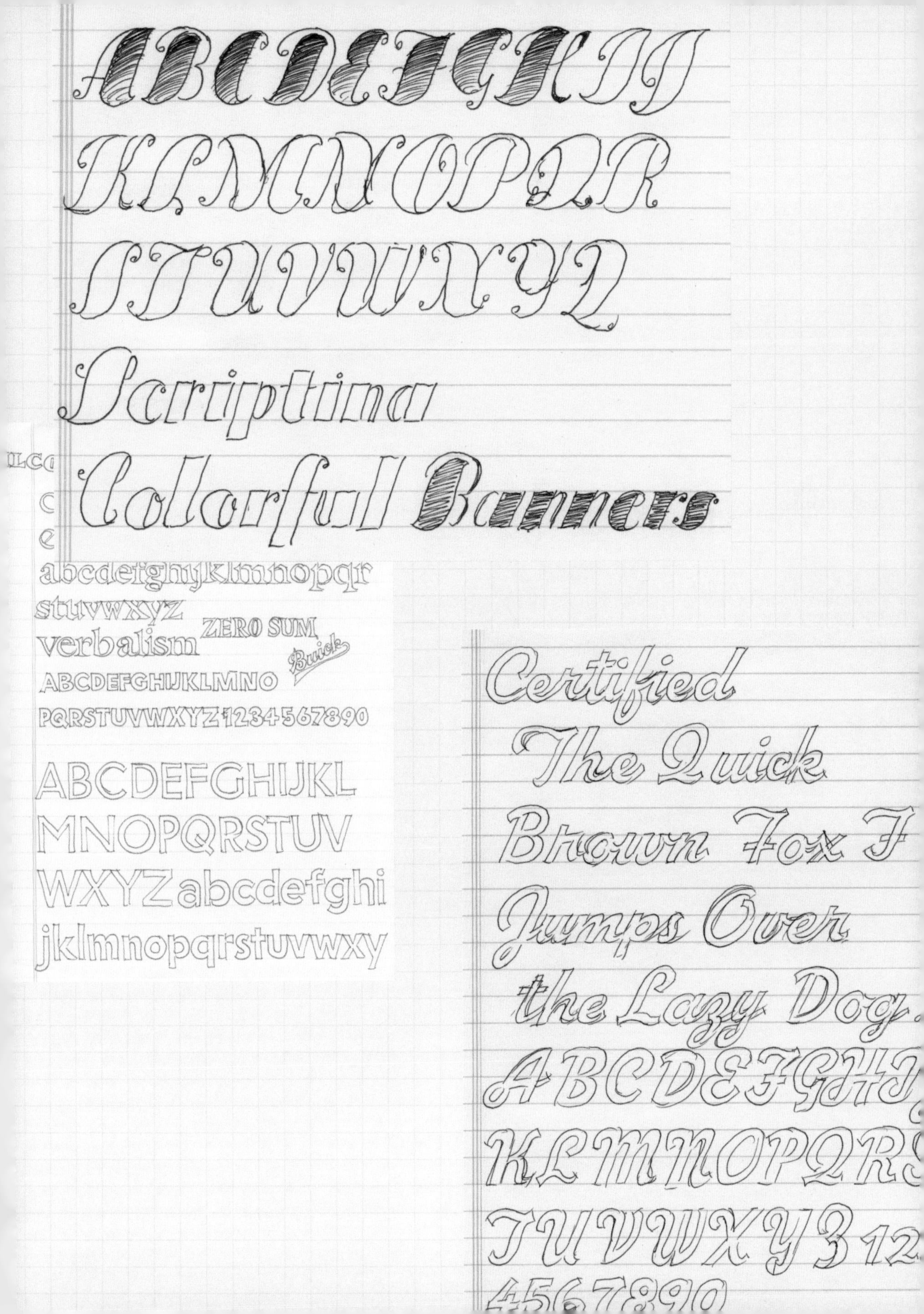

ABCDEFGHIJ

KLMNOPQR

STUVWXYZ

Scriptina

Colorful Banners

abcdefghijklmnopqr
stuvwxyz
verbalism ZERO SUM
Buick
ABCDEFGHIJKLMNO
PQRSTUVWXYZ1234567890

ABCDEFGHIJKL
MNOPQRSTUV
WXYZabcdefghi
jklmnopqrstuvwxy

Certified
The Quick
Brown Fox F
Jumps Over
the Lazy Dog.
ABCDEFGHI
KLMNOPQR
TUVWXY3 12
4567890

Ko Sliggers

Paris · France

Sketching has always marked the start of any project for chef-turned-typeface designer Ko Sliggers. 'Sometimes in a very immediate way,' he says, 'because I use the sketch in the final work. I discovered that by retracing sketches the finished work loses a lot of impact, so I use it mostly to develop an idea.'

Ko notes that sketching has its own dynamics: 'You begin to visualize an idea. The drawing hand begins as an obedient partner, but becomes autonomous and reacts to unconscious impulses, the characteristics of the surface on which you draw or the instrument you use. It is very adventurous, a kind of laboratory of the idea/concept/dream/narrative.'

The sketches shown here come from a range of drawing surfaces, from sketchbooks to beer mats. The line patterns (above and opposite),

Ko explains, are meant to be suggestive of falling rain. 'Painting them quickly and repeatedly reminded me of exercises I did at art school, a kind of *écriture automatique*. The moving brush on the paper became a challenge to surprise myself in varying the most simple forms – dot and line – to produce the raw material (the flour, if you like), from which I baked the final shapes, characters and images.'

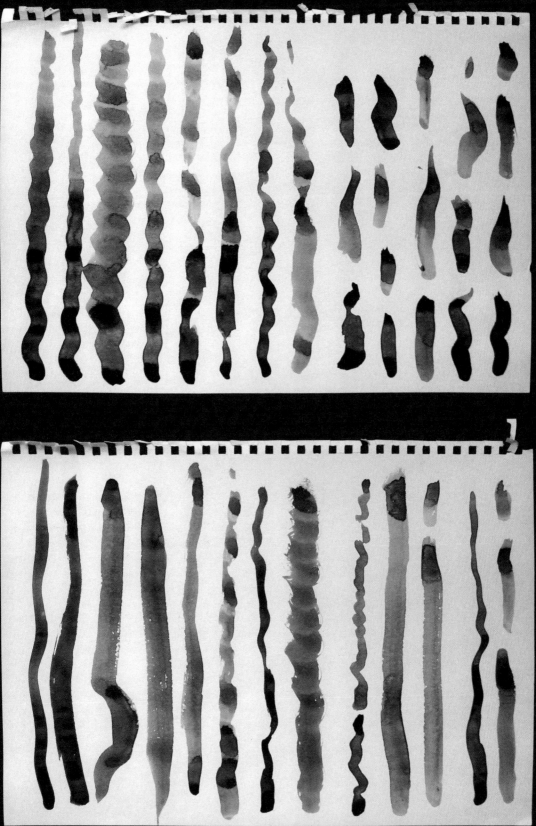

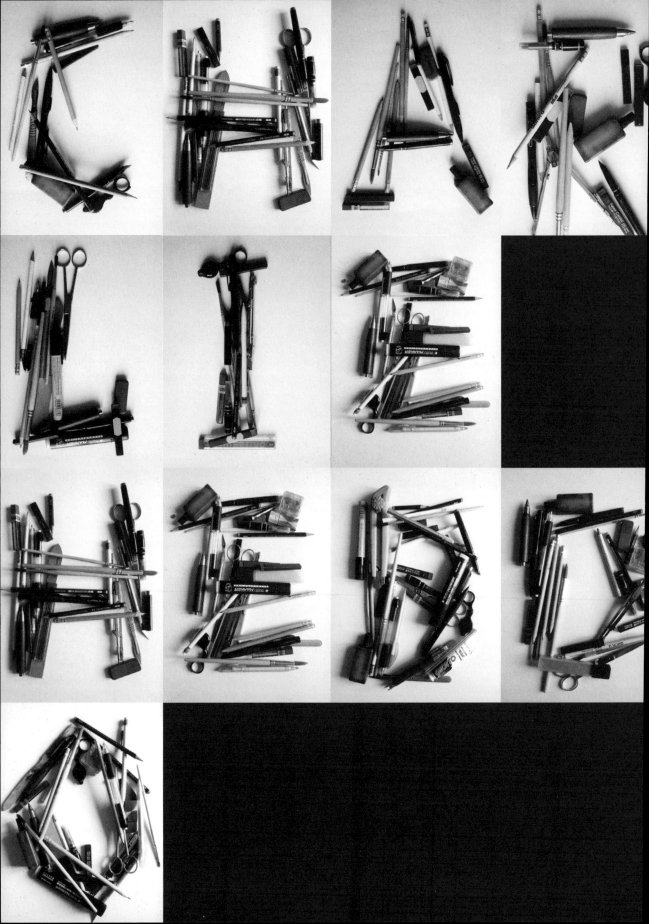

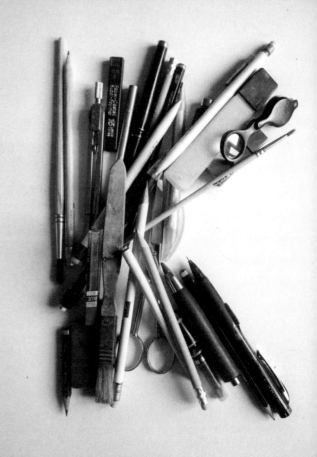

George Triantafyllakos

Thessaloniki • Greece

Working 'somewhere between design and technology', type designer George Triantafyllakos's ideals tend to evolve directly on the computer screen. But, he says, 'I've always considered sketching to be an excellent medium for externalizing knowledge and shaping ideas. A sketch is the first and most important tool of any type of design work, including type design.'

He continues: 'I am one of those designers who limits its use to the very first stages of my work, primarily as a tool to organize and focus my thoughts in certain design directions. I only do really basic design work when sketching, nothing that could be used as an intermediate product of the final work.'

As the computer screen is his design tool of choice, George only occasionally uses sketchbooks for initial drawings and ideas. He does concede, however, how 'the near-instant way one can make changes to a design and test different variations makes sketching an amazing tool for experimentation and live-testing important decisions'.

George concludes by saying that, 'I wouldn't say that the screen is any different from paper. It's just another medium that helps you materialize your thoughts. Yes, the result of this process is closer to the final product by definition, since both products (digital sketch and final file) reside on the same medium: the computer. But that is just an incidental benefit of the whole process. I believe that the choice of tool one decides to use will eventually depend on how at ease the designer is with the inner mechanics of it.'

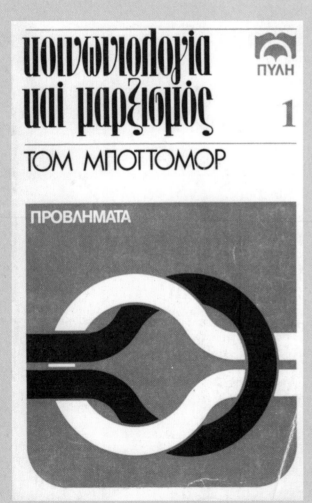

ΛΕΣΧΗ
ΣΜΗΝΙΤΟΝ

ΓΕΝΙΚΟΝ ΧΗΜΕΙΟΝ ΤΟΥ ΚΡΑΤΟΥΣ
— ΠΑΡΑΡΤΗΜΑ ΒΟΛΟΥ —

ΜΠΙΦΤΕΚ

Liron Lavi Turkenich

Haifa • Israel

Typeface designer and researcher Liron Lavi Turkenich begins the design process by sketching very freely, and only later decides which elements to pursue. In these preliminary sketches, she develops other ideas and writes notes that, she admits, are a bit messy, 'but it's a mess I understand. Those hand-drawn sketches have qualities that take a while to achieve digitally.'

'When designing a typeface, I usually take a stroke or a curve I'm especially happy with from those initial sketches, and bring it to the beginning of the digital stage,' she says.

Liron admits that although she never learned how to draw, she did discover that sketching letterforms gave her the same 'meditative activity' that drawing usually does. She prefers the combination of a soft and hard pencil, as both enable her to choose those parts that need to be emphasized and those that serve more as a background.

The sketches illustrated here show 'Aravrit', a typeface that combines Hebrew and Arabic letters – with Arabic on the upper half of the letterform and Hebrew below. With this lettering system, she says, 'one can read one's own language, without ignoring the other, which is always present. Finding a balance between the fun and quirky shapes and legibility was a challenge that I enjoyed very much.'

Of the drawing shown on p. 326, Liron explains, 'I was trying to design a lettering piece inspired by Didone typography. Because of the heavy contrast, the Hebrew letters would have a very thin "leg" and would appear to fall off. I was trying to introduce the ball of the "A" and see how things developed from there.'

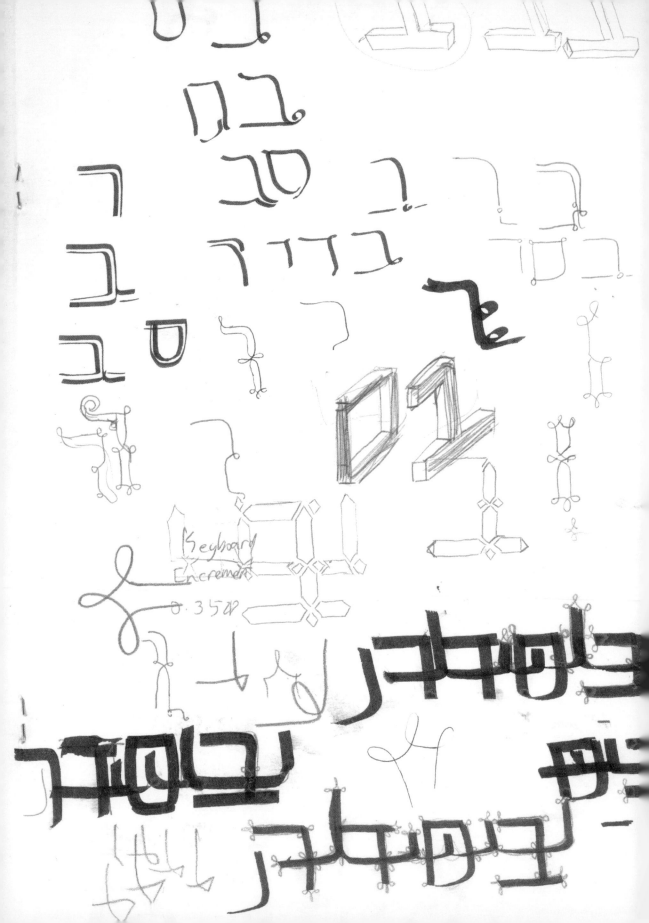

Keyboard
Encrement
0.35 ??

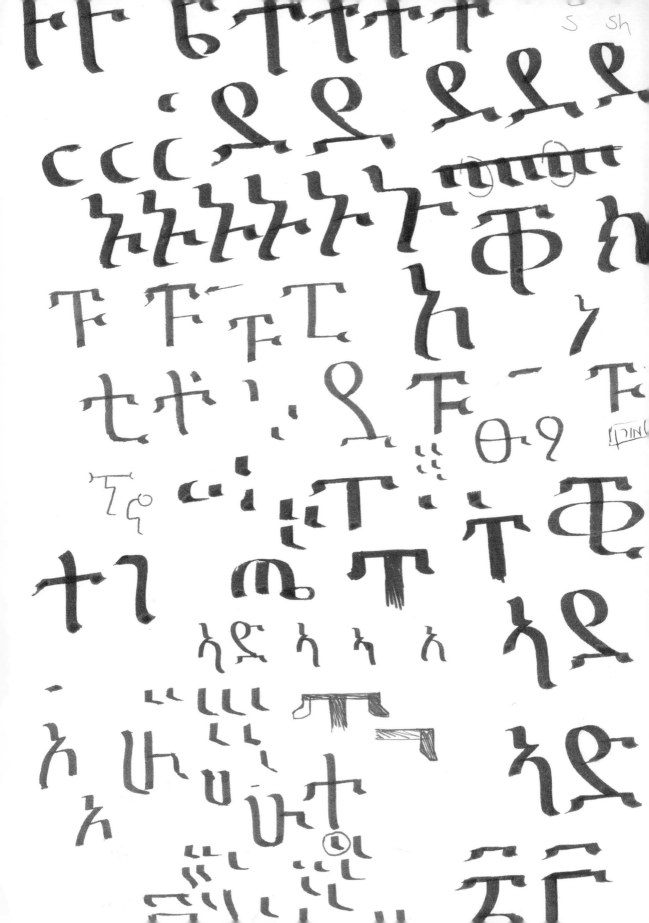

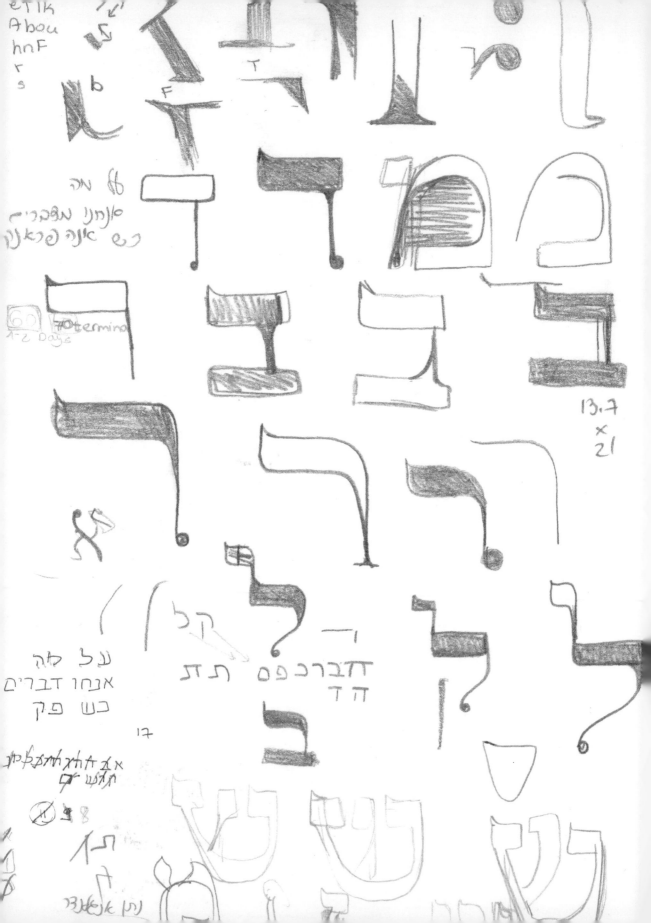

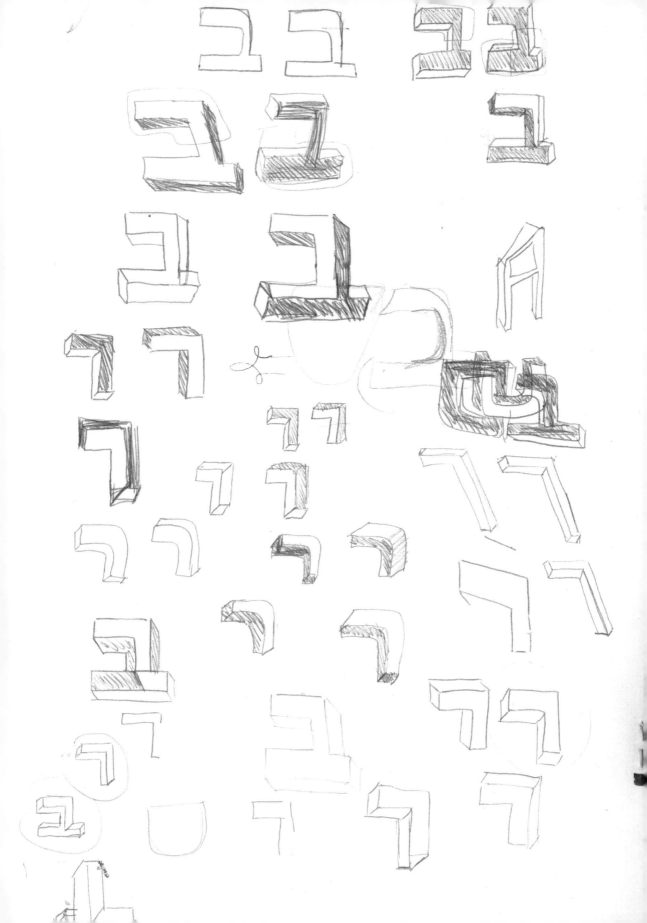

Panos Vassiliou

Athens · Greece

Sketching used to be a relaxing pastime for Panos Vassiliou, who founded the Parachute type foundry in 1999, but now its only function is to help him design particularly demanding letterforms and shapes, mostly for italics or letterforms with a handwritten or calligraphic feel.

'Sketching does help me to get a few basic letters correctly designed at the beginning of a project, including those that are more difficult, such as Zeta and Xi,' he says. 'There are several steps in this process. Some of the early rough sketches become more refined, and are the ones I try to get as close as possible to with the finished version on the computer. From then on, letters with related letterforms are designed onscreen.'

In some cases, he continues, as with the 'Regal' and 'Champion Script' typefaces, he will sketch 'many more letters than usual, owing to the distinct personality and shape of some of the letters, such as Lambda, Phi and Xi'.

Panos always begins with a 'wireframe', a single line that gives him the basic shape of the letter.

It is the step that follows – filling up the character from this rough initial stage to its full volume – which provides a welcome break from contending with Bézier curves on a daily basis.

'Apart from that, I find sketching on paper more relaxing and less stressful than drawing on a computer,' he says. 'I prefer pencils and brushes, and I haven't spent enough time learning how to use computer-simulated sketching tools. I can think of one reason I would embrace these tools, however, and that would be the ability to erase and redo a sketch at the speed of light.'

>I

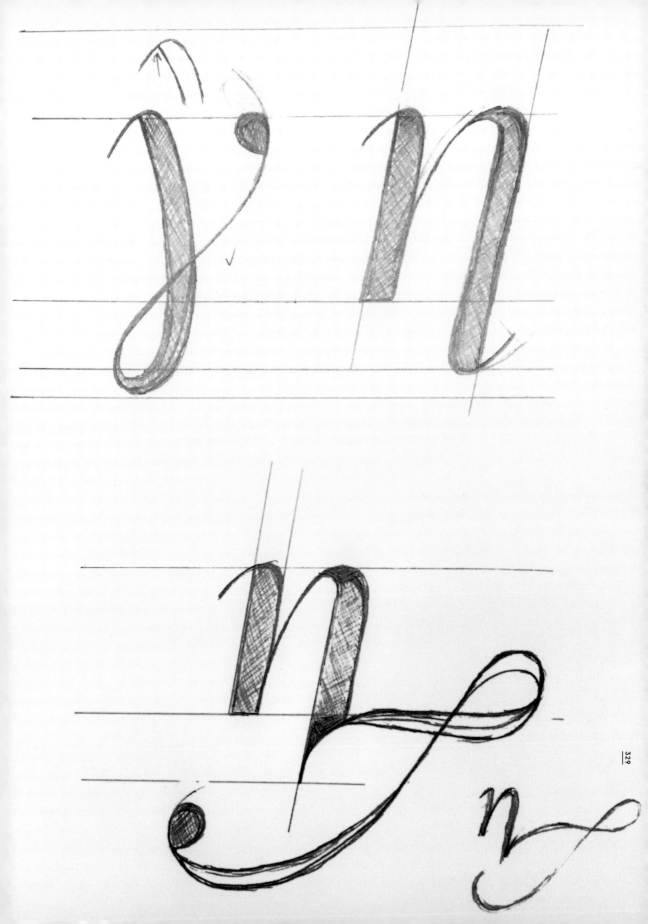

329

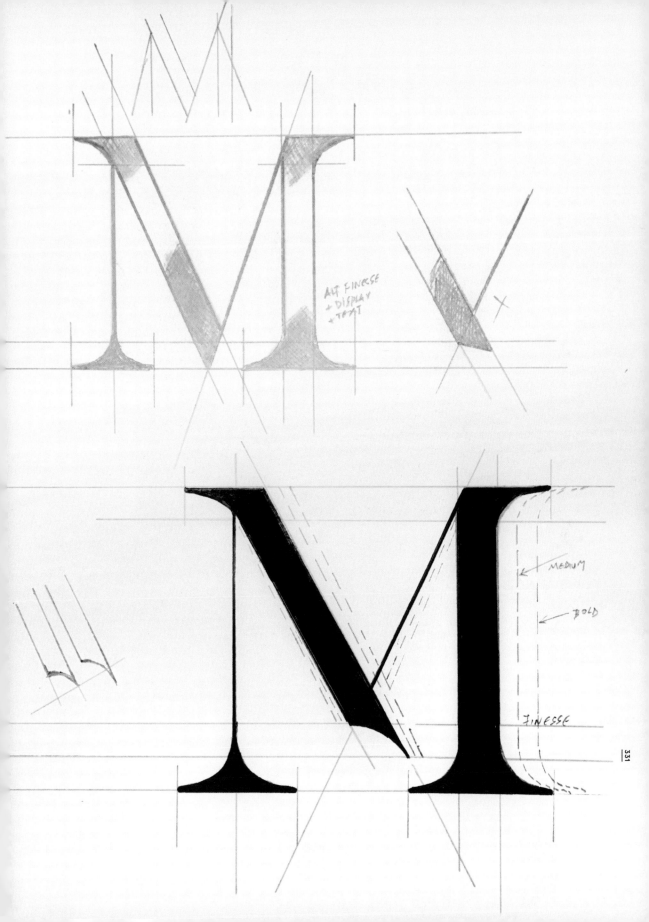

ALT FINESSE
+ DISPLAY
+ TEXT

MEDIUM

BOLD

FINESSE

Irene Vlachou

Athens · Greece

'Sketching is always done as a means to work out the balance of shapes and the desired rhythm,' explains Irene Vlachou, senior type designer at TypeTogether. 'Details and decisions about style are also decided at the drawing stage. Apart from being an important tool in my work, sketching is also an enjoyable process, being both playful and relaxing.'

Irene's tools of choice are parallel pens, calligraphy pens and, for the last couple of years, a wooden calamus, a hangover from her Arabic calligraphy classes. 'Usually I draw on a clean roll of paper, running along my desk,' she says, 'but there are times when a sketchbook seems more appropriate, especially if I'm on the go, or if I need more rigid guidelines for drawing.'

Shown here are drawings for her 'Colvert' typeface, a collaborative project for Typographies.fr, back in 2012. 'I remember trying to figure out the shape of the curly terminals of the letters Zeta, Xi, etc, and I became drawn into the process,' Irene recalls. 'I began trying out different ideas that, of course, didn't correlate to the project at all. This went on for a couple of days, but fortunately I received an email reminding me of the tight deadline we were on, and I went back to working on the actual project.'

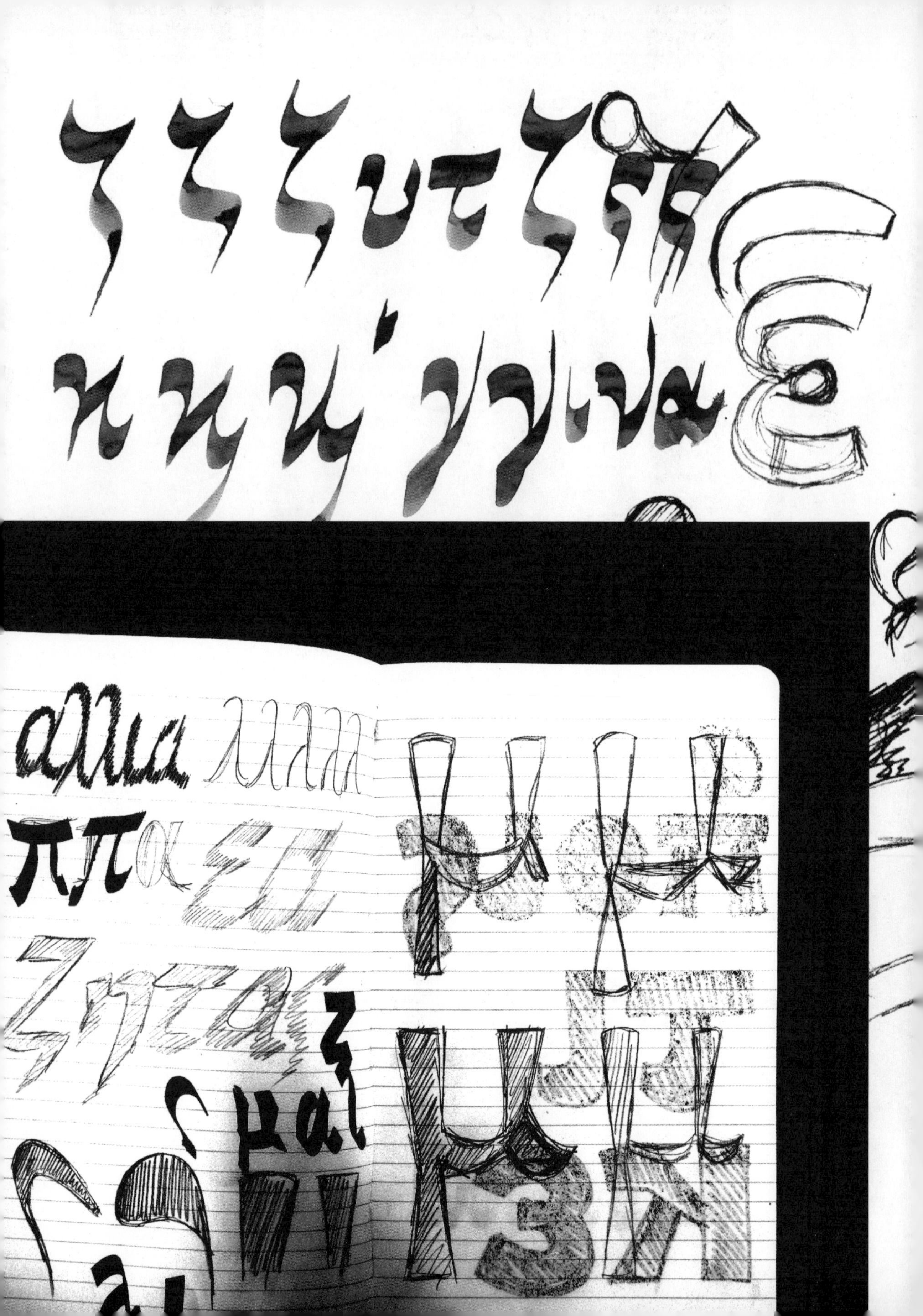

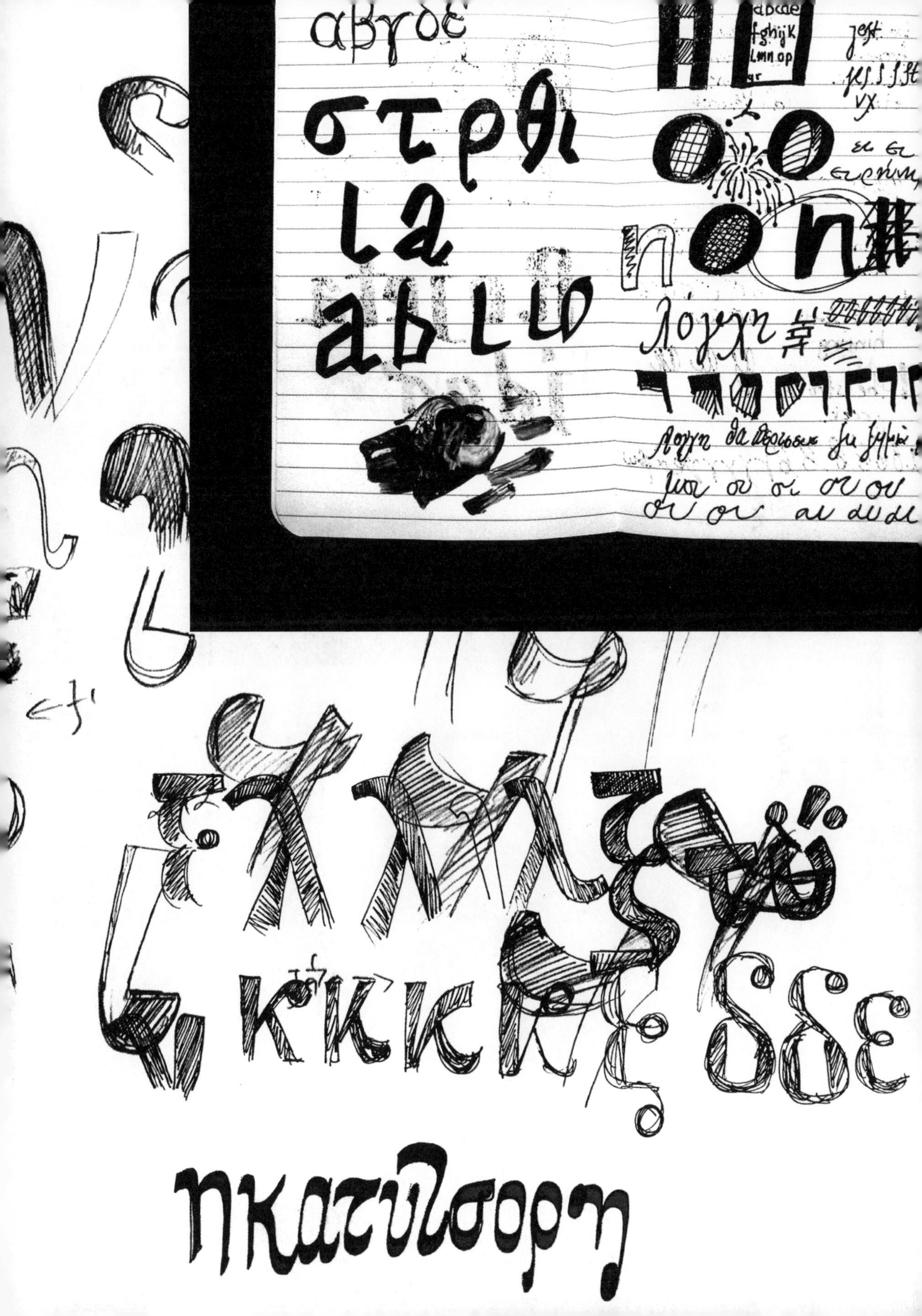
λόγχη

Terrance Weinzierl

Grand Rapids • Michigan • USA

'A paragraph of notes could be summed up in a drawing of a single letter,' says lettering artist Terrance Weinzierl, a typeface designer at Monotype. 'I don't draw analogue as much as I should, or in a habitual way, but when inspiration strikes, it pours out quickly and stops just as fast.'

Becoming too sterile, or void of details owing to the inherent geometric qualities of software drawing tools, is a common problem with digital work. 'I work back and forth between digital and analogue drawing,' Terrance says. 'Sketching makes my finished work richer with detail and personality.'

He finds that drawing on paper allows him to focus on the design without the barrage of notifications alerts appearing on his computer screen. 'It's meditative, and offers huge variety, along with some welcome restrictions,' he explains. 'Staring at an infinite Photoshop canvas makes me seize up. For the "Canton" typeface, I created two stages of drawings, many months apart. It's a great example of how you can come back to an idea and have some DNA to start with.'

Terrance admits that he runs out of patience with true ink and metal tools, and prefers brush and broad nib markers. 'Some calligraphers might think that unauthentic,' he says, 'but it's more about capturing ideas and forms than about making finished work. My computer is great at helping me to create polished pieces.'

He also maintains an official sketchbook and a daily planner, and uses plain index cards for all kinds of things. 'I'm pretty organized, with colour-coding, bullets and subheads,' he says. 'The "cocktail-napkin drawing" might be a cliché, but it's not a myth.'

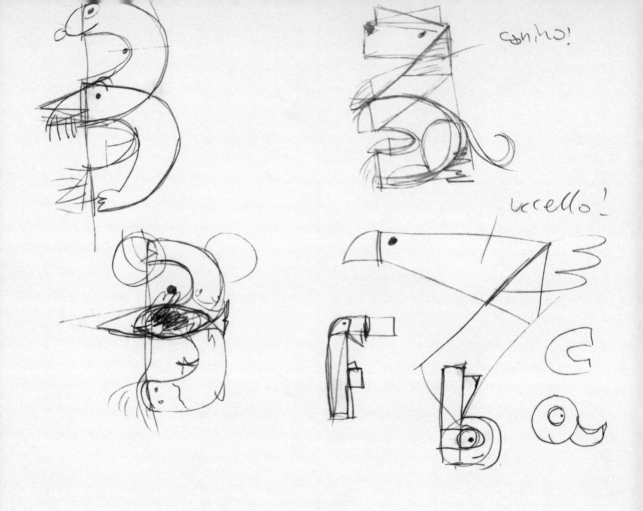

Francesco Zorzi

Amsterdam • Netherlands

Having studied in Milan and Oslo, designer and illustrator Francesco Zorzi relocated to Amsterdam in 2012 to set up the multidisciplinary design studio No Rocket. He makes his own sketchbooks, explaining that 'it's not a matter of choosing the perfect paper, because I love sketching even on poor-quality paper. It's about giving my drawings a different personality. The more uncomfortable and distracted I am, the better they are.'

Francesco enjoys the freedom of expression that he experiences while sketching: 'I can experiment without being obliged to be perfect,' he says. His tools are rudimentary: thin felt-tip pens. 'I try to be consistent in using a sketchbook,' he says. 'They are a sort of diary of my days and ideas and doodles.' The project shown here, '36 Days of Type', began on Instagram as an online space for designers and illustrators to express their views on letters and numbers, one letter a day, once a year.

'When I began, it was nearly the end of the project, with only the numbers left,' Francesco says. 'So I started with an idea for the number 5. It was extremely simple, based on two shapes, which then became something completely different as I added elements over the main grid. The result was a dog-shaped 5.'

He continues: 'Unfortunately, that first sketch is the only one I didn't keep, I designed it quickly on a piece of paper just to have something for going digital with the intermediate pencil-and-iPad step, and then lost it. But that idea gave me a method for pushing and forcing my creative process forward quickly. Over the following days, I was able to design the other numbers with the same spirit, using the same layered concept.'

3 месяц 2016
марта

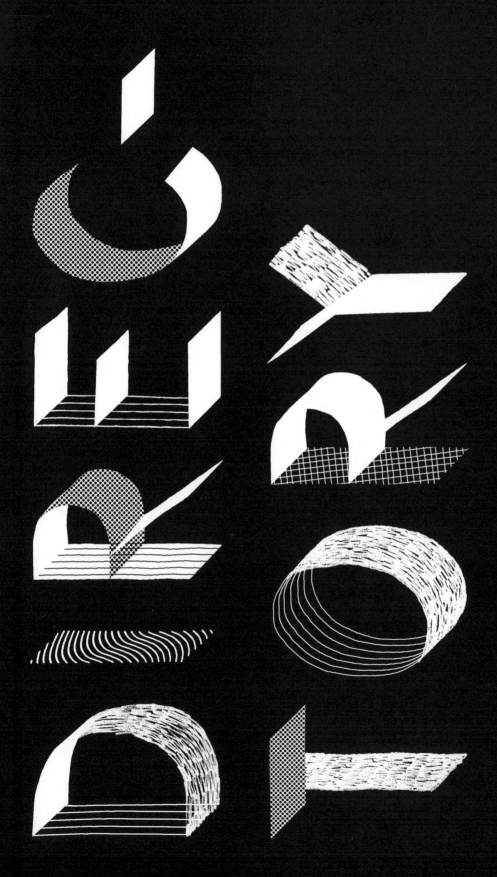

Majid Abbasi [8]
twitter.com/studioabbasi
instagram.com/studioabbasi
studioabbasi.com

Coca Albers [10]
instagram.com/coca1002
cocaalbers.com

Kelli Anderson [16]
twitter.com/kellianderson
instagram.com/kellianderson
kellianderson.com

Philippe Apeloig [22]
apeloig.com

Andrea Arcangeli [28]
behance.net/andrearcangeli

Tarek Atrissi [32]
twitter.com/atrissi
instagram.com/atrissi
atrissi.com

Peter Bankov [36]
bankovposters.com

Gabriel Benderski [40]
twitter.com/g_benderski
instagram.com/iamkiwithefruit
benderski.design
iamnotmyinspiration.com

Ed Benguiat [44]
houseind.com/hi/ed_benguiat

Julie Bjørnskov [48]
instagram.com/juliebjornskov
juliebjørnskov.dk

Benoît Bodhuin [52]
twitter.com/benoitbodhuin
instagram.com/benoitbodhuin
bb-bureau.fr

Sophie Elinor Brown [56]
twitter.com/sophieelinor
instagram.com/sophie_elinor
sophieelinor.com

Franco Cervi [60]
twitter.com/279editions
279editions.com

Nadine Chahine [62]
twitter.com/arabictype
instagram.com/arabictype
arabictype.com

Kritbodee Chaicharoen [64]
twitter.com/kritbodee
instagram.com/_kritbodee_
kritbodee.com

HanJu Chou [68]
instagram.com/gracechou1992
cargocollective.com/hanjuchou

Xavier Dupré [72]
xavierdupre.com

El Fantasma de Heredia [78]
flickr.com/photos/elfantasmadeheredia

Bahman Eslami [82]
twitter.com/besmin
instagram.com/bahmanwashere

Vera Evstafieva [86]
web.stagram.com/vera.evstafieva
facebook.com/vera.evstafieva

Oded Ezer [90]
twitter.com/odedezer
odedezer.com

Pablo Ferro [96]
pabloferro.net

Njoki Gitahi [100]
twitter.com/njokigitahi
njokigitahi.com

Milton Glaser [106]
twitter.com/themiltonglaser
instagram.com/miltonglaserinc
miltonglaser.com

Baruch Gorkin [110]
twitter.com/baruchgorkin
baruchgorkin.com

Giuseppe Del Greco [112]
beppedelgreco.com

Viktor Hachmang [118]
instagram.com/viktorhachmang
viktorhachmang.nl

Dirk Hagner [122]
dirkhagnerstudio.com

Jonathan Hoefler [128]
twitter.com/hoeflerco
instagram.com/hoeflerco
typography.com

John Holmstrom [132]
johnholmstrom.com

Indian Type Foundry [134]
twitter.com/itfoundry
instagram.com/itfoundry
indiantypefoundry.com

Yanek Iontef [140]
twitter.com/yanekiontef
instagram.com/yaneki
fontef.com

Damoon Khanjanzadeh [144]
twitter.com/damoonkhk
instagram.com/damoonkhanjanzadeh

Dmitry Kirsanov [150]
kirsanov.com

Sylvia (Di) Kong [156]
instagram.com/sylviadikong

Alexandra Korolkova [160]
nicetype.ru

Irina Koryagina [166]
twitter.com/ir1s
instagram.com/irinananana
irinakoryagina.com

Henrik Kubel [172]
a2-type.co.uk

Tom Lane [174]
twitter.com/gingermonkey_tl
instagram.com/gingermonkey
gingermonkeydesign.com

James Lunn [180]
twitter.com/n_n_u_l
instagram.com/n_n_u_l
nnul.co.uk

Pete McCracken [186]
twitter.com/crackpress
instagram.com/crackpress
petemccracken.com

Pablo A. Medina [190]
instagram.com/pablo4medina
designisculture.com

Laura Meseguer [194]
twitter.com/laurameseguer
instagram.com/laurameseguer
laurameseguer.com

Niels Shoe Meulman [198]
instagram.com/nielsshoemeulman
nielsshoemeulman.com

Thomas Milo [204]
twitter.com/thomasmilonl
decotype.com

Flavio Morais [208]
twitter.com/flavmo
flaviomorais.net

Bill Moran [212]
twitter.com/hamiltonwoodtyp
instagram.com/hamiltonwoodtype
woodtype.org

Dmitri Moruz [216]
twitter.com/dmoruz
instagram.com/dmoruz
dmoruz.com

Joachim Müller-Lancé [220]
twitter.com/kamedesign
kamedesign.com

Morag Myerscough [224]
twitter.com/moragmyerscough
instagram.com/moragmyerscough
studiomyerscough.com

Sander Neijnens [230]
twitter.com/letterbeeld
letterbeeld.nl

Jovan Shpira Obradovic [234]
behance.net/tcfd

Jayme Odgers [240]
twitter.com/jaymeodgers
jaymeodgers.com

Toshi Omagari [246]
twitter.com/tosche_e
instagram.com/toshiomagari
tosche.net

Slávka Pauliková [250]
twitter.com/typetypo
instagram.com/slavkapaulikova
slavkapaulikova.com

Judith Poirier [254]
lachoseimprimee.com

Carolyn Porter [258]
twitter.com/porterfolio
carolyn-porter.com

Dan Reisinger [262]
danreisinger.com

Dan Rhatigan [266]
twitter.com/ultrasparky
instagram.com/ultrasparky
ultrasparky.org

Bud Rodecker [270]
twitter.com/budrodecker
instagram.com/budrodecker
budrodecker.com

Mamoun Sakkal [276]
twitter.com/mamounsakkal
sakkal.com

Kristyan Sarkis [280]
twitter.com/kristyansarkis
instagram.com/kristyansarkis
kristyansarkis.com

Stephen Savage [286]
twitter.com/savageartist
instagram.com/savageillustrator
stephensavage.net

Bijan Sayfouri [290]
instagram.com/bijan.sayfouri
sayfouri.com

Jeff Scher [296]
twitter.com/fezfilms
instagram.com/jeff_scher
fezfilms.net

Zachary Quinn Scheuren [298]
facebook.com/zacharyquinnscheuren

Goeun Seo [302]
instagram.com/goeun_seo
goeunseo.com

Mohammad Sharaf [306]
twitter.com/mohammadrsharaf
instagram.com/mohammadrsharaf
mohammadsharaf.com

Mark Simonson [312]
twitter.com/marksimonson
marksimonson.com

Ko Sliggers [316]
dutchfonts.com

George Triantafyllakos [320]
twitter.com/georgetrianta
backpacker.gr

Liron Lavi Turkenich [322]
twitter.com/lironlavitur
lironlavi.com

Panos Vassiliou [328]
twitter.com/parachutefonts
flickr.com/groups/parachutefonts
parachutefonts.com

Irene Vlachou [332]
twitter.com/typetogether
instagram.com/type_together
type-together.com

Terrance Weinzierl [336]
twitter.com/typeterrance
instagram.com/typeterrance
typeterrance.com

Francesco Zorzi [340]
instagram.com/fra_z
francescozorzi.it

Much thanks to Lucas Dietrich, our editor and
friend, along with sincere appreciation to Elain
McAlpine, Alex Wright, Kate Thomas, Ella-Kate
Whitehead and all at Thames & Hudson for
their efforts on this project.

The book is about the beauty of and passion
for letters, typefaces and drawing. Thank you
to our wonderful contributors for allowing us
to peek into your processes. We know some
of you would rather not expose the insides of
your closets and drawers, but you did, which
doubles our gratitude.

We are also grateful to David Rhodes,
President, and Anthony Rhodes, Executive Vice
President, of the School of Visual Arts (SVA) in
New York, where type, type design and lettering
of all kinds is at the core of an incredible
amalgam of design programmes.

Free Hand: New Typography Sketchbooks
© 2018 Steven Heller and Lita Talarico

First published in the United Kingdom
in 2018 by Thames & Hudson Ltd,
181A High Holborn, London WC1V 7QX

Published in 2018 by Abrams, an imprint of
ABRAMS. All rights reserved. No portion of this
book may be reproduced, stored in a retrieval
system, or transmitted in any form or by any
means, mechanical, electronic, photocopying,
recording, or otherwise, without written
permission from the publisher.

ISBN 978-1-4197-3107-5
10 9 8 7 6 5 4 3 2 1

Printed and bound in China

Abrams books are available at special discounts when
purchased in quantity for premiums and promotions
as well as fundraising or educational use. Special
editions can also be created to specification. For
details, contact specialsales@abramsbooks.com or the
address below.

ABRAMS The Art of Books
195 Broadway, New York, NY 10007
abramsbooks.com